I0449894

# Hidden in the Shadow of Truth

# Hidden in the Shadow of Truth

*Why Our Black Boys Choose Criminality, Prison, and Enslavement*

Reginald E. Hicks

## Hidden in the Shadow of Truth
### Why Our Black Boys Choose Criminality, Prison, and Enslavement

*Copyright © 2010 by Reginald E. Hicks*

*All rights reserved. No part of this book may be used or reproduced by any means, graphic, electronic, or mechanical, including photocopying, recording, taping or by any information storage retrieval system without the written permission of the publisher except in the case of brief quotations embodied in critical articles and reviews.*

*Grateful acknowledgment is made for permission to use or reprint the following: Excerpts from* Before Freedom, *edited by Belinda Hurmence. Copyright 1990 by John F. Blair, Publisher. Excerpted by permission of the publisher.*

*iUniverse books may be ordered through booksellers or by contacting:*
*iUniverse*
*1663 Liberty Drive*
*Bloomington, IN 47403*
*www.iuniverse.com*
*1-800-Authors (1-800-288-4677)*

*Because of the dynamic nature of the Internet, any Web addresses or links contained in this book may have changed since publication and may no longer be valid. The views expressed in this work are solely those of the author and do not necessarily reflect the views of the publisher, and the publisher hereby disclaims any responsibility for them.*

*ISBN: 978-1-4502-1667-8 (pbk)*
*ISBN: 978-1-4502-1668-5 (ebk)*
*ISBN: 978-1-4502-1669-2 (hbk)*

*Printed in the United States of America*
*iUniverse rev. date: 5/11/10*

*To my wife, Brenda, and my daughter, Miea,*
*for their unwavering love, encouragement, and support.*

*To my father and mother, William and Gloria Brown,*
*for raising me in the way that I should go.*

*To my grandparents, Edgar and Ellen Saunders,*
*for always being the cornerstone of our extended family.*

*To my brother, Stacey Hicks, and my sister, Sabrina Roberts,*
*for always being my brother and sister.*

# Contents

# Preface

As a black male educator and a fifteen-year veteran of the public school system, I have been a teacher, a counselor, and a mentor to students of many different hues, backgrounds, and statuses. And yet it is the attitudes and behaviors of many of my black male students that have caused me the most concern. It is their unprovoked aggressiveness, their unrelenting negative outlook, their lack of investment in their own education, and their glorification of prison life that left me, year after year, with a single burning question that I finally had to answer for myself: why do our black boys *choose* enslavement? That is, why do many of them *choose* the path of incarceration through criminality? For me to ignore this question would have been to admit an unqualified indifference to the social health of our community and to the future of our people. We can no longer afford to bury our heads in the sand while our sons and brothers enthusiastically embrace failure, prison, and death.

*Hidden in the Shadow of Truth* is the result of my determination to inform the ill-informed and lead the misled out of the darkness of propaganda, lies, and half-truths. I truly believe that knowledge is a necessary prerequisite to healing. Our black boys cannot be helped if the ailment is not understood. If I neglect to share what I have learned after two years of painstaking research and fifteen years of observations and interactions in the classroom, then I have failed in my duty and role as a responsible educator. Likewise, we all have a duty to do whatever we can to cut the ties that bind and enslave our black boys. *Hidden in the Shadow of Truth* was not written to prescribe solutions for "the black male problem." That task must be left to the innovative minds of dedicated community leaders like Dr. Princella Johnson of Eastern Virginia's Millennial Mentoring Youth Academy, Dr. Steve Perry of Connecticut's Capital Preparatory Magnet School, and Dr. Geoffrey Canada of Harlem Children's Zone Promise Academy Charter Schools. I undertook this project primarily to challenge conventional wisdom and provide a comprehensive and clear understanding of the social issues affecting the outcomes of our black male children. Surely, knowledge is only one element in the long process of healing, rehabilitation, and progress, but as any physician would certainly attest to, it is absolutely the most important element. Please read this book and share its contents as we help each other to help our people.

# Introduction:
# The Plantation of Choice

*Who is more foolish, the child afraid of*
*the dark or the man afraid of the light?*

—Maurice Freehill

Who would *choose* poverty over wealth, sickness over health, or slavery over freedom? Who would *willingly* sacrifice all that they have (liberty and integrity) for a "mess of pottage" and the selfish aims of another? Who would trade family and community, opportunity and success, for what some have characterized as "a nigger's paradise"[1]—*prison*? How some have answered these questions, through words or deeds, may be surprising. From the mouths of four former North Carolina slaves (among others) interviewed in the 1930s, the following excerpts are very telling:

> No slaves run away from Marster. They didn't have
> any excuse to do so ... Marster loved his slaves, and other
> white folks said he loved a nigger more than he did white
> folks ... We stayed on with Marster after the war ... We
> lived in the same place until Old Marster and Missus

died. Then we lived with their relations right on and here. I am now on a place their heirs own.[2]

I think slavery was a mighty good thing for Mother, Father, me, and the other members of the family, and I cannot say anything but good for my old marster and missus, but I can only speak for those whose conditions I have known during slavery and since. For myself and them, I will say again, slavery was a mighty good thing.[3]

I had good owners, all of them. My masters never did hit me. Missus would not whup me much. She just wanted to show off sometimes ... When they told me I was free, I didn't notice it. I stayed on and worked just like I had been doing, right on with Missus and Master. I stayed there a year after the surrender.[4]

I was kept at the big house to wait on Miss Polly ... Miss Polly made us niggers mind, and we had to keep clean. My dresses and aprons was starched stiff. I had a clean apron every day ... One day my mammy come to the big house after me. I didn't want to go, I wanted to stay with Miss Polly ... I looks back and thinks. I ain't never forgot them slavery days, and I ain't never forgot Miss Polly and my white starched aprons.[5]

There are several ways that one might explain this seemingly nostalgic yearning for previous conditions of servitude. Some might posit that those who were treated relatively well on the plantation were easily socialized to believe that "Marster and Missus" had only their best interest at heart, and the fact that they were enslaved was inconsequential.[6] Others may logically assume that because these former slaves were interviewed in the 1930s, in the midst of the Great Depression (1929–1941), even slavery seemed more bearable than their current struggles.[7] And still a few may speculate that nineteenth-century slaves were so far removed from their African homeland that many succumbed to the propagandized rationale for their own enslavement: that slavery, as ugly as it was, saved them from savagery, idolatry, and damnation by giving them the "gift" of Christianity.[8] Whatever the reason, these voices suggest an "irrational attachment" to what can be considered an abomination of human history—the oppressive chattel slavery of the antebellum South.

I intend to show that this "irrational attachment" to slavery did not end with the Negro slave of the nineteenth century, but continues with the African American slave of the twenty-first century. The oppressive chattel slavery of the antebellum South may have been extirpated by the Civil War and the Thirteenth Amendment, but the *humanitarian plebeian slavery* (explained in the next section, *Slavery Defined*) of the U.S. prison system remains alive and well, and is now—in 2008—the "plantation of choice" for nearly one million black men in the United States. Although blacks account for just 13 percent of the U.S. population, the one million blacks that are incarcerated represent 41 percent of the penal slave system.[9] Whites, on the other hand, account for 66 percent of the U.S. population and only 37 percent of the penal slave system.[10] The Hispanic numbers are 15 percent and 19 percent, respectively.[11] The only conclusion that can be drawn from these sobering facts is that the black male population has a greater attachment to slavery (i.e., the U.S. prison system) than any other racial or ethnic group. This "irrational attachment," I contend, is developed through a unique socialization process that does not necessarily predestine one to criminality, but certainly makes one more prone to it, which means that "choice" is still a factor. My goal, then, is to analyze this socialization process and provide some explanation as to why so many of our black boys develop a peculiar, undaunted affection for the penal slave system, leading directly to their tendency to choose enslavement through criminality. More specifically, I intend to focus on the influences of the four basic agencies of socialization: (1) the family of orientation, (2) the school system, (3) the child's peer group, and (4) the mass media. Before we consider these issues, however, we must first answer the paramount question: can the U.S. prison system be defined as an "authentic" institution of slavery?

## Slavery Defined

In one form or another, slavery has been part of the human experience since the dawn of civilization. From the slaves who built the grandiose temples of Egypt and excavated the brimming silver mines of Athens, to the twenty-seven million "new" slaves of the twenty-first century who are victims of bonded labor, trafficking, and forced marriages, slavery has assumed myriad forms. In 1842, Henry Wadsworth Longfellow, an American-born poet and a product of the European Romantic movement, eloquently described, in verse, one of the most recognizable forms of slavery—a form of slavery illustrated by what American Southern aristocrats of the time self-righteously referred to as "our peculiar institution":

Beside the ungathered rice he lay,
His sickle in his hand;
His breast was bare, his matted hair
Was buried in the sand.
Again, in the mist and shadow of sleep,
He saw his Native Land.

...

He did not feel the driver's whip,
Nor the burning heat of day;
For Death had illumined the Land of sleep,
And his lifeless body lay
A worn-out fetter, that the soul
Had broken and thrown away![12]

Frederick Douglass, a man born and bred in the muck and mire of this so-called peculiar institution, railed against his illegitimate birthright:

Learning to read ... had given me a view of my wretched condition, without the remedy. It opened my eyes to the horrible pit, but to no ladder upon which to get out. In moments of agony, I envied my fellow-slaves for their stupidity. I have often wished myself a beast. I preferred the condition of the meanest reptile to my own... I often found myself regretting my own existence, and wished myself dead; and but for the hope of being free, I have no doubt but that I should have killed myself, or done something for which I should have been killed.[13]

Both Longfellow and Douglass describe an iniquitous system of degradation and servitude that represents one of the best historical examples of slavery. In that world, the enslaved were as much property as a pack mule or a prized steed, and it was not uncommon for an animal to receive better treatment than a slave. In fact, slaves were not allowed to be away from their owner's premises without permission, nor could they be taught to read or write. They were not permitted to marry, make contracts, or own property. And the status of a slave was determined by that of his mother, so that if his father was free (whether he was a former slave or a white slave master) and his mother was enslaved, his lot would be enslavement.[14] This, in short, is the oppressive chattel slavery of the antebellum South. But is this the only representative model of slavery? What of other historical examples?

One of the earliest of written records that makes a clear reference to an established system of slavery is the Code of Laws compiled during the reign of Hammurabi (1795–1750 BC) over the world's first metropolis, Babylon in Mesopotamia. Written in cuneiform script (the earliest known form of written expression), King Hammurabi laid down 282 case laws, of which no less than twenty-five dealt with issues of slavery and the rights and obligations of slaveholding. An analysis of the Babylonian "slave code," juxtaposed to that of the nineteenth-century American slave system, shows that even within seemingly analogous institutions, there can be significant differences in the circumstances and treatment of the enslaved. In accordance with the laws of Hammurabi, the slaves of Babylon were not only permitted to marry, but they could marry into any status, slave or free, wealthy or poor. They could set up housing with their spouse, enter into business, accumulate wealth, and buy fixed property. "Nevertheless, even by this humanitarian code, the slave was still considered merchandise,"[15] so that any privileges granted by the state were contingent upon the acquiescence of the slaveholder. In fact, the code makes it clear that the slave was prohibited from leaving the owner's premises without explicit permission and that anyone who found a slave "in the open country" was obligated to return the runaway to his master, upon which time the finder would receive a nominal reward for his services.[16] This concept of "slave treated as property" might be considered a common theme until one reads the Code of the Hittites.

The ancient kingdom of the Hittites (c. 1650–1100 BC) extended from Asia Minor and northern Syria to the western fringes of Mesopotamia. In tandem with Hammurabi's Babylonia, the Nesilim (the Hittite people) also had an established system of slavery supported by an intricate code of laws. The Code of the Hittites rivaled the Code of Hammurabi in its specified treatment of the enslaved. Whether a slave was purchased in the open market, acquired through military conquest (the predominant method of acquisition), or enslaved pursuant to a punishment for committing a heinous crime against the state, the Hittite "slave code" was very specific about the fair treatment of this class of people. Like the slaves of Babylon, Nesilim slaves were free to marry whomever they wished. They could enter into business, accumulate wealth, buy fixed property and, in some cases, purchase their own freedom. Unlike the slaves of Babylon, however, Nesilim slaves, although certainly considered inferior, were not treated as "property." In fact, the Hittite code of laws contained many clauses in which the slave was required to be treated as a person. In other words, his life and bodily integrity were to be protected, and any interaction he had with his master (even if a law was violated by the slave) was normally mitigated by reason, common sense, and morality.[17] One cannot assume, then, that chattel slavery (slaves treated as property), albeit common, is necessarily an indispensable characteristic of an *authentic* slave system.

This brief historical comparison tells us that there are clear distinctions between (1) the *oppressive chattel slavery* of early nineteenth-century America, (2) the *humanitarian chattel slavery* of Hammurabi's Babylon, and (3) the *humanitarian plebeian slavery* of the Hittites. *Oppressive chattel slavery* refers to a system of exploitation where the enslaved have no basic human rights and are treated as property. In *humanitarian chattel slavery*, the enslaved are granted certain specified privileges (limited human rights) by the state but are still treated as property. And under *humanitarian plebeian slavery*, slaves are not only allowed certain rights and privileges, but the law requires (with some stipulations) that they be treated as people. These obvious differences tell us that the forms of slavery and the circumstances and treatment of the enslaved are protean factors based on time period, culture, region, and venue. The same cannot be said, however, about the word *slavery* itself. I contend that although slavery has many faces, its universally applicable definition remains unchanged. This point may become more obvious as we consider the "new" slavery of the twenty-first century—a more pervasive and insidious form of servitude that has supplanted the universally eradicated (as of 1970, with the exception of Mauritania) traditional chattel slavery of the past.

Comparing the old and new forms of slavery is like the cliché of comparing apples to oranges. Both apples and oranges share a common label (*fruit*) with a universal definition (*the ripened, edible, seed-bearing part of a plant*), even though they are starkly different in shape, color, and consistency. For example, the transatlantic African slave trade (begun by the Spanish in 1502) was precipitated by several factors: (1) the strong European demand for the prized tropical crops (cotton, sugar, tobacco, molasses, and rum) of the New World (the new European colonies of the time) that could not be grown in Europe, (2) the unusual expansion of landownership in the New World and the subsequent perpetual need for cheap labor, and (3) a ready source of "durable," inexpensive bondsmen via a preexisting indigenous African slave trade perpetuated by Africans themselves.[18]

The new slavery (twenty-first-century slavery), on the other hand, was born out of contrastingly different circumstances. The first contributing factor was the dramatic increase in the world's population since the end of World War II (1945), which has tripled from about two billion people to over six billion, the greatest part of that increase occurring in countries where slavery is most prevalent today (mostly in what are considered developing countries). This population explosion not only put a detrimental strain on the resources of particular countries, but it increased the supply of potential slaves while decreasing the cost of acquisition, giving these potential bondservants a character of *disposability.*

The second contributing factor was the rapid shift in developing countries from small-scale farming (the predominant support structure of the poor) to cash-crop agriculture, which precipitated a massive displacement of peasants, who were driven from their land and forced to seek employment in the cities, making these untold millions economically vulnerable to potential enslavement.[19]

The final contributing factor was government corruption. "Just having large numbers of vulnerable people doesn't automatically make them slaves."[20] Only corrupt "keepers of the peace" working in conditions of anomie under weak central governments can provide the impetus needed to put into place an international illegal slave trade that has reached such prodigious proportions—an estimated twenty-seven million people enslaved around the world.[21] This new form of slavery focuses on short-term, quasi-legal (not supported by law) ownership of ethnically diverse slaves who are inexpensive, disposable, and require very little, if any, maintenance. Conversely, the old slavery focused on long-term, legal ownership of ethnically similar slaves who, as major investments, had to be constantly monitored and maintained. But whether one is the victim of the old or new forms of servitude, under oppressive or humanitarian conditions, treated as chattel or plebeian, the definitions of *slave* and *slavery* remain static and completely immutable. So how does one go about defining these universally applicable terms?

We must first turn to etymology. *Slave* is derived from the Latin word *sclavus*, referring to the many Slavs (Slavic-speaking people of Eastern Europe) sold into slavery beginning in the early ninth century by conquering peoples.[22] According to *The*

*Random House Dictionary of the English Language* and the *Online Etymology Dictionary*, the word *slave* first surfaced as a part of the English language (Middle English) around 1290, spelled *sclave* and defined as "a person who is the property of another." This is the first fundamental characteristic of slavery: *implied ownership*. Most historians, anthropologists, economists, and sociologists tend to agree that service without implied ownership is something other than slavery.[23] Even the plebeian slave of the Hittites, although not *treated* as property, was as much property as the chattel slave of early nineteenth-century America because, like all slaves, they too were defined by their lack of free will. To hold countless numbers in bondage (as property), however, has always been simply a means to an end. In fact, throughout human history, the enslaved have performed a variety of functions for their malevolent sponsors, propelled by a presumption of ownership. They have served, usually without pay, as builders of cities, harvesters of crops, excavators of mines, soldiers of war, and servants of households, among a host of other uncompensated services that have, historically, placed a premium on their being defined as property. This lends itself to our second fundamental characteristic of slavery: *rigid exploitation*.

*The American Heritage Dictionary* defines *exploitation* as "the utilization of another person for selfish purposes." This is the essential element of the arrangement between master and slave. Under Roman law, for example, the slave was "but a thing serving as a medium for the master's aims."[24] Ownership, then, in and of itself, is not slavery. The primary motivating factor of any form of slavery is the benefit achieved from the service provided.[25] For instance, "most European colonial economies in the Americas from the sixteenth through the nineteenth century were dependent on enslaved African labor for their survival."[26]Of course, the rigid exploitation of Africans during this time not only led to the survival of burgeoning colonial economies, but it elevated Brazil to the world's leading producer of sugarcane during the sixteenth and seventeenth centuries; it allowed Saint Dominique (later, Haiti) to surpass Brazil in sugar production by the eighteenth century; and it made America's antebellum South the Cotton Kingdom of the western hemisphere by the nineteenth century. But how does one maintain such a system of ownership and exploitation that is so antithetical to the natural human tendency to want freedom? The answer to this question is the third fundamental characteristic of slavery: *physical confinement.*

Physical confinement refers to a restriction of movement[27] and maintenance of the slave state through *social control.* According to sociologists, social control is any and all methods used to promote conformity to required norms.[28] Physical confinement through social control is the only way to explain why lucid, rational-minded people with a natural aversion to servitude would docilely accept their own enslavement for indefinite periods of time. In other words, social control involves an *internal* (psychological) and an *external* (physical) process of promoting conformity and obedience. The slave state of mind, therefore, is not innate; it is developed through a thorough subjection to effective methods (e.g., violence, fear, and deception) of social control. From the slave who received fifty lashes for not responding to his Christian name, to the slave who is violated and tortured for refusing to accept her role as prostitute, violence is one of those effective methods that has been used as a tool for slave maintenance in virtually all forms and venues of slavery.[29] The same also holds true for fear and deception. Fear, of course, is a natural outgrowth of violence. It is fear that makes violence an effective method of social control. Deception, on the other hand, is a means of socializing the enslaved with the notion that their enslavement is justified. This has been done by using religious fatalism (e.g., bondage as a vehicle for "*saving* the savage"), restricting subversive information, manipulating an incurred debt (the basis of bonded slave labor of the twenty-first century), severing family ties, and the slaveholder promoting himself as the slave's only benefactor. As such, it is these three tools of social control—violence, fear, and deception—that have ensured the physical confinement of the slave and the maintenance of the slave system.

So, based on our first three fundamental characteristics, how do we define *slavery*? Slavery is *a system of (1) rigid exploitation engendered by the (2) implied ownership of (3) physically confined people.* Most historians, sociologists, and anthropologists would be content with such a sound and universal definition, but I contend that there is one final essential characteristic of slavery that speaks directly to the viability of any slave system. That is, no form of slavery has ever existed without the voluntary or involuntary[30] submission (a total loss of free will) of the enslaved. If every potential slave, past and present, reflected the same rebellious demeanor as Gabriel Prosser (1800), Denmark Vesey (1822), and Nat Turner (1831), slavery would have never existed, and the word *slavery* would have never found its way into our lexicon.

In other words, one who refuses to serve the aims of the master might be beaten, tortured, sold, or even killed, but without exploitation, he is not a slave. As we have already established, slavery is not slavery without exploitation, and exploitation cannot occur without the voluntary or involuntary submission of the enslaved. *Full submission*, then, is the fourth fundamental characteristic of slavery and the final element of our comprehensive, universal definition: *a system of (1) rigid exploitation engendered by the (2) implied ownership of (3) physically confined people who have (4) fully submitted (voluntarily or involuntarily) to the will of the exploiter.* Using this definition as a basis, it would not be difficult to determine that the 80,000 slaves of the ancient Greek city-state of Athens, the 25 million slaves of the Holy Roman Empire, the 4 million slaves of the antebellum South, and even the 27 million "new" slaves of the twenty-first century are all part of "authentic" slave systems. But what about the 2.4 million people currently incarcerated in America's prison system? Can "prison" be considered "plantation"?

## Prison as Plantation

One would certainly be remiss to assume that the primary *manifest function* (serving a recognized or intended purpose) of prison is anything other than "[to confine people] for safe custody while on trial for an offense or for punishment after trial and conviction."[31] Be that as it may, I intend to show that the myriad prisons and jails in the United States are all part of an institution that exploits a physically confined, fully submitted, state-owned population, making it an "authentic" slave system. Ironically, this purported system of servitude is supported by the very same constitutional amendment (the Thirteenth Amendment) that many felt was the fulfillment of the promise of "liberty and justice for all" found in the Declaration of Independence. The Thirteenth Amendment (1865) states: "Neither slavery nor involuntary servitude, *except as a punishment for crime, whereof the party shall have been duly convicted*, shall exist within the United States …"[32] (emphasis added). This historic amendment not only leaves countless prison populations unprotected (aside from the protections of the First, Eighth, and Fourteenth Amendments),[33] but it also actually precipitates their enslavement—assuming, of course, that *prison as plantation* is not nonsensical. That is, assuming that the U.S. prison system exhibits each of the four fundamental characteristics of slavery: (1) physical confinement, (2) implied ownership, (3) full submission (voluntary or involuntary), and (4) rigid exploitation.

*Physical confinement* is the most conspicuous characteristic of slavery exhibited by modern-day penal institutions. Before the American Revolutionary period (1776–1789), prisons or jails were used mainly for the confinement of debtors who could not meet their obligations, of accused persons waiting to be tried, and of convicts who were waiting for their sentences of death or banishment to be put into effect.[34] The idea of using confinement, itself, as a standard form of punishment did not become widely accepted in the United States until the last decade of the eighteenth century, corresponding directly to the work of John Howard (a prison reformer) in England, to the prison reform act of 1790, and to the building of the Walnut Street Jail (considered to be the first modern prison in the United States) in Philadelphia, also in 1790. The American Revolution, therefore, ushered in a new role for the U.S. prison system and a revised statement of its purpose: to confine people for safe custody while on trial for an offense *or for punishment after trial and conviction*. This new function—based on the premise that if the state isolates the criminal from the ranks of law-abiding citizens, the amount of crime in society will diminish[35]—makes *imprisonment* and *confinement as punishment* synonymous concepts.

In accordance with the mandates of the Federal Bureau of Prisons (an oversight and enforcement agency established in 1930), convicts are confined in one of three types of federal correctional facilities, based on the assessed level of threat to public safety, corrections staff, and other inmates. The first type of facility is maximum or high-security prison, also known as the U.S. Penitentiary (USP). USPs generally hold inmates who have committed serious crimes, such as murder, robbery, kidnapping, treason, or other felonies, justifying the strictest methods of social control and confinement. Some of these methods include: (1) "twenty-three-hour lockdown" in a single cell with one hour reserved for showers and exercise in the cell block or an exterior cage; (2) limited, strictly controlled movement using physical restraints and a correctional officer escort; (3) high stone walls or reinforced fences with electronic detection devices and powerful spotlights; and (4) armed tower guards who monitor the prison grounds twenty-four hours a day. For those who require greater controls and total separation, even beyond what is provided by maximum or high-security prisons, supermaximum prisons (developed during the mid-1980s) may be the only other option.

The second type of facility is the Federal Correctional Institution (FCI), used to house medium- and low-security inmates, most of whom are convicted of misdemeanors (e.g., assault and petty theft) and are considered less dangerous than maximum-security prisoners. FCIs sometimes resemble campuses where inmates live in dormitories or in private rooms that are locked at night and are directly supervised by a correctional officer. During daytime hours, FCI prisoners have some freedom of movement and conditional access to educational and athletic facilities. They are also required to participate in work and treatment programs as a part of their confinement. FCIs are usually secured by a double-fence perimeter with an electronic detection system and armed tower guards or roving patrols.

The third and final type of federal correctional facility is minimum-security prison, or the Federal Prison Camp (FPC), where inmates convicted of nonviolent crimes, such as forgery, tax evasion, perjury, and obstruction of justice, are confined. Because these inmates are least likely to flee or commit violent acts, FPCs are the most open and least restrictive type of prison. They include non-secure, monitored dormitories, little supervision or control of inmate movement within the prison, and limited or no perimeter fencing.

In the federal prison system, therefore, the methods used in limiting movement and preventing escape—essential elements of physical confinement—are inextricably tied to the class of inmate represented in the prison population. But whether one is incarcerated in federal, state, or private prisons, in city or county jails, under maximum-, medium-, or minimum-security conditions, it is blatantly apparent that physical confinement is, in fact, the most conspicuous characteristic of slavery exhibited by modern-day penal institutions.

Can a similar argument be made for *implied ownership*? Are convicts considered *property of the state*? There can be no gainsaying of the facts that convicts *do not* have full constitutional rights; that Congress has given prison officials full discretionary control over prisoner classification (i.e., placement in maximum-, medium-, or minimum-security facilities); and that the courts have, in many cases, deferred their authority over the rights and treatment of prisoners to the leadership of the prison system itself.[36] Nonetheless, just as there are no *legal* sanctions for the ownership of the 27 million global slaves of the twenty-first century, likewise, evidence of the implied ownership of the 2.4 million inmates in the U.S. prison system is not dependent on the approbation of the U.S. Constitution, the Congress, the state legislatures, or the courts. One need only show the complete submission (one of the four fundamental characteristics of slavery) of the confined to the dominating influence of those who maintain their confinement.[37] Full submission (a total loss of free will) is not only a necessary precondition for exploitation, but it is also a natural prelude to ownership. Free will must be extinguished before ownership can be established. So, again, are convicts considered property of the state? Is free will deliberately extirpated in the process of de-socializing new prisoners?

In *Restorative Justice in Prisons* (2006), Kimmett Edgar and Tim Newell make it clear that the traditional duty of any prison is to maintain social control by denying prisoners the right to make decisions for themselves (denying free will), demonstrating the dominance of the state over the offender. For example, prisoners are told where to reside within the prison itself. They are given limited options in choosing diet, apparel, and job assignments. Their contact with family and friends is limited, regulated, and monitored. And they are required to submit to any request made by prison authorities, such as random drug testing, indiscriminate body searches, and personal property raids.[38] Inmates are, therefore, subjected to rules governing every aspect of life, which means that privacy and free will do not exist in the prison environment.[39] As such, to be "deprived of freedom of action or expression"[40] goes beyond mere confinement. Confinement involves limiting movement and preventing escape (the deprivation of *freedom* only), but having complete control over behavior (the deprivation of *freedom of action*) is the foundation of implied ownership. From this we must conclude that convicts are, in fact, property of the state. So, the U.S. prison system is certainly an institution that consists of a physically confined, fully submitted, state-owned population. But, as aforementioned, slavery is not *authentically* slavery without *rigid exploitation*.

To utilize another person for selfish purposes with little or no compensation (exploitation) is the primary function of any form of slavery, the prison plantation being no exception. The only distinction that must be made is that penal institutions serve two primary functions: a *manifest* primary function (serving a recognized or intended purpose), and a *latent* primary function (serving an unrecognized or hidden purpose). The primary manifest function of prison is to confine people for safe custody while on trial for an offense or for punishment after trial and conviction—physical confinement. The primary latent function is rigid exploitation, the evidence of which reaches deep into the annals of American history, beginning with the earliest prisons in colonial days. For instance, on December 2, 1773, in the mountains of the British colony of Connecticut, one of the most deplorable conceptions of human history was given life. A cold, abandoned copper mine of the early 1700s was converted into a prison work camp called the "Simsbury dungeon." "During the day, convicts worked above ground making nails, barrels and shoes. At night, they were confined below ground in dank, [poorly ventilated], claustrophobic caverns ..."[41] The conditions of this facility were so horrific that the Connecticut prison became notorious even abroad. Today, after the Bill of Rights (1791), the Fourteenth Amendment (1868), the creation of the American Correctional Association (1870), the Federal Bureau of Prisons (1930), Federal Prison Industries (1934), and the National Correctional Industries Association (1941), and after the landmark Supreme Court ruling in *Cooper v. Pate* (1964), the conditions and treatment of inmates have undoubtedly improved. But because inmates are still coerced to participate in prison work programs[42] (even when labeled as voluntary) and earn only 20 to 30 percent (or less) of what is earned on the outside for similar services,[43] they remain a vulnerable source of cheap labor. Thus, the notion that the inmate is but a thing (property) serving as a medium for the master's aims permeates the very foundation of the U.S. prison system.

Prison work programs (i.e., prison industries, work release programs, or staff support programs within the prison itself) are generally supported by the widely accepted and reasonable view that "inmates who are confined in corrections institutions should work as hard as the taxpayers who provide for their upkeep"[44] which is why nearly every eligible inmate in most U.S. correctional facilities participates in some form of productive labor. This was the overriding philosophy of the Federal Bureau of Prisons (BOP) when it created Federal Prison Industries (UNICOR) in 1934. As an employer of more than 21,000 inmates (approximately 11 percent of the federal prison population), UNICOR is one of the largest consumers of convict labor in the United States. Since its inception, it has generated more than 700 million dollars in revenue from its many lucrative industries (e.g., manufacturing office furniture, processing recyclable materials, producing electronic equipment and components, etc.), and yet UNICOR pays its inmate laborers less than $1.20 per hour for their services.[45] Many state prison industries generate more than 20 million dollars *annually* from convict labor and still pay their inmates less than $2.20 (this figure represents a standard policy where inmates may keep no more than 20 percent of their wages) per hour.[46] No one of competence or credibility would argue that incarceration should be an enjoyable experience or that prisoners should repay their debt to society through sloth and idleness. Likewise, no lucid, rational-minded person would presume an absence of exploitation where a physically confined, fully submitted, state-owned population is coerced to produce millions of dollars in revenue while receiving meager, inequitable compensation for services rendered.

These findings can only lead to one possible conclusion: that *prison as plantation* is not nonsensical—that the U.S. prison system is, without question, an *authentic* institution of slavery, albeit *humanitarian* (slaves having some basic rights granted by the state) and *plebeian* (slaves treated as inferior but not as property) in nature. Making this connection between enslavement and incarceration is like sweeping old territory with a new broom. The idea that "penal servitude [is] a new incarnation of slavery"[47] is nothing new. The Thirteenth Amendment (1865) itself gave states the legal authority to define the convict as a slave and treat him as such. Many states even incorporated the Amendment's stipulation into their respective constitutions to give further credence to their use of slavery and indentured servitude as a punishment for crime.[48] It is not surprising, then, that in 1871 a Virginia appellate court would use the language of slavery in its ruling against a convict plaintiff in *Ruffin v. Commonwealth*:

> For the time, during his term of service in the penitentiary, he is in a state of penal servitude to the State. He has, as a consequence of his crime, not only forfeited his liberty, but all his personal rights except those which the law in its humanity accords to him. He is for the time being a slave of the State. He is *civiliter mortus*; and his estate, if he has any, is administered like that of a dead man. The bill of rights is a declaration of general principles to govern a society of freemen and not of convicted felons and men civilly dead.[49]

This bold condemnation is endemic of the hands-off relationship that existed between the courts and prisons at least until the landmark Supreme Court case *Cooper v. Pate* (1964) was decided—a case that in effect affirmed that prisoners do have some basic civil rights "guaranteed" by the U.S. Constitution.[50]

Nonetheless, when the rights of prisoners conflict with the proper functioning of the correctional facility, the courts will almost always defer to the discretionary authority of prison officials.[51] So, as with any other form of slavery, any rights bestowed upon the enslaved are in most cases dependent on the acquiescence of the slaveholder, which means that the slave (i.e., the convict) has no rights that can be considered absolutely guaranteed. Such is the penal slave system, destined to be the *chosen* fate of 1 in 3 of our black boys, and has been the *chosen* fate of 1 in 5 of their fathers.[52]

In the post-bellum South during the time of the black codes, one could argue with impunity that the imprisonment of black people was primarily the result of entrapment or unjust laws. But in the twenty-first century one would have to search far and wide to find even a handful of such cases. The fact is, according to the U.S. Department of Justice Statistics (2006), although blacks represent only 13 percent of the U.S. population, they commit 42 percent of all violent crimes—a proportion that neatly reflects the 41 percent of blacks in prison. They commit 51 percent of all murders, 32 percent of forcible rapes, 56 percent of robberies, and 34 percent of aggravated assaults.[53] The overarching question is, *why* are we losing so many of our black males to criminality and a twenty-first-century slave institution?

My contention is that many black boys embody debilitating personality flaws (environmentally induced pathologies) that are developed through a unique socialization process, making them more prone to choosing a path leading directly to prison. Some of these pathologies include: (1) a negative view of "blackness," resulting in the devaluation of one's own life; (2) a lack of self-confidence, leading to a suppression of potential talent and ability; (3) an overemphasis on immediate satisfaction, to the detriment of long-term success; (4) a warped sense of manhood, defined by *over-aggression* and *extreme machismo* and (5) an antiquated, unhealthy hatred and paranoia of white people. My goal in the following four chapters is to investigate how these personality flaws are developed through the four basic agencies of socialization: (1) the family of orientation, (2) the school system, (3) the child's peer group, and (4) the mass media. The concluding section focuses on why these personality flaws make black males more prone to choosing enslavement through criminality. In a real sense, my hope is that through a better understanding of the socialization of our black boys, we can begin the process of healing our communities and eradicating the veiled stigma of prison being "a nigger's paradise."

# 1

# The Influence of the Family

*It is easier to build strong children*
*than to repair broken men.*

—Frederick Douglass

In terms of children learning to participate successfully in group life, the *family of orientation* (the family we are born into) is the first and most important agency of socialization. "The child's first exposure to the world occurs within the family."[1] It is within this parent-based agency of socialization that the child is provided with a name, an identity, and a heritage. Parents introduce the child to his first set of norms, values, and beliefs; they help him form some of his basic attitudes and modes of behavior; and they directly contribute to the development of his self-concept and ultimate personality.[2] If parents offer love and approval, the child learns to love himself. If parents offer rejection, the child learns to dislike who he is. If parents offer encouragement, the child learns to be confident. If parents offer criticism, the child learns to be unsure. If parents offer hostility, the child learns to be violent. And if parents offer serenity, the child develops peace of mind. It is no wonder that of all the agencies of socialization, the family has the single greatest influence on the outcomes of children. So, when 60 percent of our black boys are reared in fatherless households (51 percent living in mother-only families and 9 percent living with neither parent)[3] and have limited or no access to positive black male role models, or when they are taught antiquated notions of a white enemy who is bent on rejecting them at every turn, it would stand to reason that their outcomes may be different than their white and Asian counterparts. Let us consider first the central, daunting issue of fatherlessness.

## Uninvolved, Absentee Fathers

What happened to the black family? In 1890, not more than twenty-five years after the last shot was fired to finally put an end to the so-called peculiar institution, 80 percent of our children lived in two-parent homes.[4] Even during the upheavals of two world wars and the Great Depression, this enviable rate remained relatively unchanged—a fact that discounts the trite argument that modern (twenty-first-century) black family structure is a direct outgrowth of the separation of families during slavery. The demise of the two-parent black family did not begin in earnest until 1970, when their numbers sank to 64 percent, followed by 48 percent in 1980, 39 percent in 1990, and 35 percent today.[5] This drastic downturn is very peculiar in light of the fact that for almost one hundred years after the Civil War, only about 20 percent of black children were raised in female-headed households.

So, what happened to the black family? Is there a reasonable explanation for this swift, unprecedented change in black family structure? Several hypotheses have been presented and examined attempting to answer these very complex questions. Three of the most prominent hypotheses are based on economic status. The first hypothesis supports the general principle that as socioeconomic status increases, the percentage of female-headed households decreases. In other words, "differences in female-headedness between blacks and whites diminish sharply under conditions of economic parity."[6] So, the percentage of black mother-only families (51 percent) compared to that of whites (18 percent) is skewed by the fact that the number of poor blacks and blacks in poverty has increased in recent years. The second and third hypotheses point specifically to the economic weakness of the black male. He earns less than 65 percent of what white men earn at every educational level, and his unemployment rate is more than double that of white men.[7] This legitimizes the claim made by many black women that there are very few "marriageable" black men available (hypothesis two) and that they would rather maintain a family on their own to remain eligible for welfare transfer payments (hypothesis three), which they could not receive if they were found to be cohabiting.[8] A fourth hypothesis suggests that "shifts in values and attitudes about marriage and childbearing in the black community have led to increased acceptance of out-of-wedlock childbearing and growth in black female-headed families."[9]

As logical and reasonable as these theories may be, neither of them can fully justify a rate of father-absenteeism that surpasses other racial and ethnic groups by 30 to 47 percent, nor can they justify the cumulative effect that such a rate has on our black boys. With only about one-third of black federal and state prisoners reporting to have been raised in two-parent homes,[10] the efficacy of fatherlessness is irrefutable (by a margin of 10 to 1, black single-parent homes are almost always female-headed). Even the vilified Moynihan Report of 1965 was prophetic in its assessment of the damaging effects of black family structure. In his capacity as assistant secretary of labor under the Johnson administration, Daniel Patrick Moynihan (an American politician and sociologist) wrote this report during a time when more than 75 percent of black children still lived in two-parent homes. His focus was on the nearly 25 percent (60 percent today) who were not so lucky. The thrust of Moynihan's argument is that the Negro family cannot fight a two-front war against poverty and racial discrimination from a position of extreme weakness—the slow deterioration of the black community through the dissolution of the two-parent black family. He makes it clear that most of the aberrant, inadequate, and antisocial behaviors exhibited especially by black boys are a direct byproduct of father-absenteeism. The mother-only black family, according to Moynihan, perpetuates crippling negatives: (1) a resentment of the son for the misdeeds of the father, (2) a blind focus by children on the immediate gratification of their desires, (3) an inability of the black child to stave off the deep psychological wounds of racism, (4) educational priorities favoring daughters over sons, (5) a suppression of basic intelligence and future school performance, and (6) a weak work ethic among black boys. To buttress his arguments, Moynihan quotes a host of social scientists throughout his report, including famed black sociologist E. Franklin Frazier, whose poignant 1950 statement in *The Journal of Negro Education* still rings true today:

As a result of family disorganization, a large proportion of Negro children and youth have not undergone the socialization which only the family can provide. Their disorganized families have failed to provide for their emotional needs and have not provided the discipline and habits which are necessary for personality development. Because the disorganized family has failed in its function as a socializing agency, it has handicapped the children in their relations to the institutions in the community. Moreover, family disorganization has been partially responsible for a large amount of juvenile delinquency and adult crime among Negroes. Since the widespread family disorganization among Negroes has resulted from the failure of the father to play the role in family life required by American society, the mitigation of this problem must await those changes in the Negro and American society which will enable the Negro father to play the role required of him.[11]

As fatherlessness in the black community has become nothing less than a national epidemic in recent years, many social scientists and researchers have joined the voices of Moynihan and Frazier, hoping to stem the tide of an obviously losing battle. A host of scholars has produced well-supported, reliable studies that have shown strong relationships between family structure and various measures of child development. One key measure of development mentioned by Moynihan that is affected specifically by the presence or absence of the biological father is *basic intelligence*, which speaks directly to the issue of overall school performance. In regard to this capacity of a child to acquire and apply knowledge (basic intelligence), the sticking point for many social scientists is not necessarily whether family structure has an effect on cognitive ability, but more often whether intelligence can be accurately and fairly measured across racial and ethic groups.

Putting aside this perpetual controversy, however, common sense informs us that despite the measurement used to assess racial/ethnic differences in intellectual development, the verbal IQ of *any* child is intimately linked to the amount of verbal stimulation received from parents, keeping in mind that it is very difficult for a single parent to provide the same amount of stimulation that can be provided by two parents.[12] Moreover, in a study of over 17,000 children, Deborah A. Dawson (1991) found that the average education of the mother was highest in families with both biological parents and lowest among mothers who never married,[13] making the quality of single-parent verbal stimulation suspect at the very least. Dawson goes further to say that "children living with single mothers or with mothers and stepfathers were more likely than those living with both biological parents to have repeated a grade of school,"[14] which is certainly partially reflective of a lack of cognitive ability among these children. In a similar study, using a National Longitudinal Survey (NLS) of 2,500 black and white respondents, Sheila Fitzgerald Krein and Andrea H. Beller (1988) discovered a strong causal relationship between a child's family type and his or her subsequent level of academic achievement—children of two-parent families, of course, experiencing the more positive result. They even found that the effect was greater for boys than for girls.[15] Such findings are neither isolated nor surprising given the many measures of development affected by fatherlessness.

As noted in *Psychology Today* (1996), "Fatherhood turns out to be a complex and unique phenomenon with huge consequences for the emotional and intellectual growth of children."[16] The same can also be said of motherhood. Both biological parents play distinct, indispensable roles in family life. Fathers and mothers parent differently, play differently, communicate differently, and certainly discipline differently. In fact, when it comes to discipline, fathers enforce the rules systematically and sternly, emphasizing consequences for right and wrong, while mothers tend toward grace and sympathy in the midst of disobedience.[17] As different as fathers and mothers are in their approaches to parenting and discipline, both are equally essential in the process of producing mentally strong, emotionally stable, mild-mannered children who are not compelled to sexual deviance or physical aggression. But because more than 90 percent of black single-parent homes are mother-headed (as opposed to father-headed),[18] and because 60 percent of black children are reared in fatherless households, it is predominantly the absence of the father that negatively impacts the *socioemotional maintenance* (promoting and maintaining feelings of unconditional love and acceptance) of black children in general and black boys in particular.

In a comparative study of incarcerated adolescent males and their nonincarcerated cohorts, M. Eileen Matlack et al. (1994) examined the correlation between family structure and the tendency toward antisocial behavior. Their findings strongly confirmed several hypotheses: (1) that incarcerated adolescents were more likely to come from mother-only families than were nonincarcerated adolescents; (2) that incarcerated adolescents exhibited greater deficiencies in social communication skills, appropriate self-expression, and effective interpersonal problem solving than nonincarcerated adolescents; and (3) that these "social skill deficits" were a direct outgrowth of father-absenteeism.[19] Likewise, using a large longitudinal sample of urban elementary school children, Nancy Vaden-Kiernan et al. (1995) observed a similar connection between family type and social behavior. The study concluded that "boys in both mother–father and mother–male partner families were significantly less likely than boys in mother–alone families to be rated as aggressive by teachers. [No such effect was found for girls]."[20]

Another measure of development highlighted by Daniel Patrick Moynihan in 1965 is a child's ability to delay gratification. This measure is not only strongly tied to family structure, but it has a significant intervening effect on emotional stability, social skill attainment, cognitive ability, academic achievement, and ultimate career success in adulthood.[21] According to Joan E. LeFebvre (2003), *self-regulation* or delay of gratification is a learned skill that begins to emerge between the ages of three and four. It involves the capability of a child to suppress short-term impulsivity while actively maintaining the behavior needed to achieve a long-term goal, without external motivation or instruction.[22] This acquired skill is essential in the lives of children, adolescents, and adults. It is one of the few natural prerequisites to long-term success. In their analysis of differential parenting styles in two-parent families, Wendy S. Grolnick and Richard M. Ryan (1989) made it clear that a child's ability to delay gratification is bolstered mainly by the mother. She spends more time actively interacting with the children and is, therefore, more involved in child rearing than the father.[23] But in the single-parent family where the father is absent, the mother's central role is irrevocably weakened due to inadequate financial and social capital.[24] In such cases, the single mother may not only be forced to work full-time outside the home, but she is also fully responsible for maintaining the household and supervising the children. So, when paternal resources (e.g., child monitoring and support) are completely absent, and the mother's time and energy are severely siphoned by her insurmountable responsibilities, it is the proper socialization of the children that inevitably suffers. The female-headed household (absent the influence of a nonresidential biological or surrogate father) is simply not conducive to a successful reinforcement of skills like self-regulation or delaying gratification. All in all, through his absenteeism, the biological father sabotages the role of the custodial parent and the development and outcomes of his children. He also denies his sons access to their first and most important role model—their own father.

## Inaccessible *Positive* Role Models

The *Encyclopedia of Sociology* and the *Dictionary of Sociology* define *role models* as people whose opinions matter to us and whose judgments are most important to the development of our self-image. From the point of view of the child, role models possess life skills and display coping techniques that the child learns by observation and comparison with his own performance. He evaluates himself based on the patterns of behavior presented by those whom he feels connected to and identifies with. In other words, role models impart to children certain norms (specific behavioral expectations), values (general cultural guidelines), attitudes, and beliefs, whether they be considered positive or negative. Role models may or may not be known personally by the child. They may include professional athletes, famous actors, government leaders, as well as teachers, classmates, or even fictitious movie characters. Nevertheless, the most influential group of role models has always been, and continues to be, the family.[25] No other *reference group* (i.e., a group of role models) can boast of a connectedness that goes beyond mere admiration or superficial affection. Because of kinship ties, family members have a vested interest in the overall well-being of the child. They tend to make a conscious effort to demonstrate to the child how to participate successfully in group life. But how effective is this effort for black boys who have less access to their primary role model (the biological father) than their sisters (whose primary role model is the mother), or their white, Hispanic, and Asian counterparts? Are black males the most effective role models for black boys strictly by virtue of their common race and gender, notwithstanding family ties?

The fact that black boys are at the bottom of the developmental totem pole, beneath all other racial, ethnic, and gender groups, is a testament not only to their estrangement from their biological fathers, but also to the differential treatment they receive from their mothers. As with any good parent, the black single mother may love her sons and daughters equally, but her child-raising practices are most certainly influenced by her individual circumstances and the genders of her children. She sees herself as the daughter's primary role model and as the son's temporary benefactor. In the female-headed household, daughters are expected to be independent-minded and follow strict rules and guidelines. They are expected to be well-behaved and respectful, to do well in school, to earn their high school diploma, and to eventually go to college.[26] No such pressure is placed on the sons. Perhaps because of their perception of black men in general and the absentee father in particular, many black mothers tend to encourage their sons to be athletes or entertainers rather than scholars.[27] In their own family of orientation, therefore, our black boys are not given the same encouragement to pursue academic excellence that is thrust upon their sisters. They are instead offered a dream (e.g., basketball or rap stardom) that by every measure, regardless of social group, is no less than a long shot, and more than 99 percent of the time is an absolute dead end.[28]

Evidence of this gender-based disparity in treatment by well-meaning black single mothers is clear and unequivocal. According to a recent *Newsweek* article (2003), more than 17 percent of young black men are high school dropouts (the culmination of dramatically lower grades and higher suspension, expulsion, and retention rates) compared to 13.5 percent of young black women; 25 percent of black males go to college, while 35 percent of black females do; and only 17 percent of black men have become part of the professional–managerial class, whereas 24 percent of black women have ascended to this level.[29] Does this mean, then, that the best role models for young black males are other black males?

Some may call it common sense or belaboring the obvious to pronounce that a child is more likely to admire, respect, and emulate a person who looks like him. But for our black boys this small bit of conventional wisdom is especially true. It is not our black girls who reject academic success and perceive it as mainly a "feminine" endeavor. It is not our girls who are disproportionately labeled as "slow learners" and are overly represented in special education programs. They are not the ones who are killing each other and who are viewed by their parents and teachers as hyperactive and aggressive. These are distinctive characteristics of young black males with limited access to positive black male role models.[30] As such, contrary to much of the existing literature, being raised in a female-headed household, in and of itself, is not necessarily synonymous with high risk and poor developmental outcomes. A growing body of evidence suggests that a high-quality relationship with the nonresidential biological father or a suitable surrogate father solicited from the extended family or local community promotes positive results and higher levels of well-being for black boys.[31] Even noted black psychologists Dr. Spencer Holland and Dr. Darlene Charles strongly support the notion that "it takes a man to properly raise a man," whether that man is the primary role model (the nonresidential biological father) or a secondary or surrogate role model.[32]

Many education specialists are also aware of the efficacy of black male role models in the lives of black male children and, in some cases, have gone so far as to advocate the creation of all-black, all-male schools directed, supervised, and taught strictly by black men. Although such an idea has many detractors (e.g., psychologist Dr. Kenneth Clark, who assisted in the landmark 1954 case *Brown v. Board of Education of Topeka*), the logic of the proposal, according to Dr. Spencer Holland, is crystal clear: "Because they have few, if any, [positive black male role models] in their non-school environment, we have to show many African-American males that education is something that men not only do, but excel in."[33] The message here is that the black community's *social fathers* (biological and surrogate) have essentially surrendered their paternal responsibilities to an already overburdened school system. But is this actually the case? Are black male role models ostensibly *missing in action*?

Nonresidential biological fathers across the board tend to give very little of themselves (financial support, emotional reinforcement, authoritative parenting, frequent visitations, and so on) to their children. According to the National Fatherhood Initiative (2007), of the 24 million children nationwide who reside in female-headed households, only about 25 percent have regular weekly contact with their biological father. The remaining 75 percent either have no contact at all (33 percent) or inconsistent contact at best.[34] This unconscionable lack of involvement among the 11 million nonresidential fathers in the United States is also reflected in the fact that the vast majority of them (over 64 percent) pay no child support to the custodial mother.[35] As they are justifiably admonished for what can be considered severely irresponsible behavior, many of these fathers emphatically contend that their noninvolvement is due to several extraneous factors: (1) they may have had no previous connubial bond with the mother and, therefore, less of an emotional attachment to the child; (2) they may have become a father at a very young age and are thus emotionally and financially unprepared for the task of fatherhood; (3) they may have a volatile relationship with the mother, directly affecting the frequency and quality of their visitations; (4) they may have spent most of their parenting years in jail or prison; or (5) they may be simply economically ill-suited to plan visits, arrange outings, or pay child support.

As a significant part of this group, nonresidential black fathers are similarly inaccessible to their children and articulate some of the same explanations. In fact, the literature is clear that black children are much more likely than white children to be born to a poor, never-married teenage mother and an economically disadvantaged father who has served some time in prison.[36] So, when a majority of black fathers live in separate residences, pay no child support, and are relatively invisible to their children,[37] the only solace that can be gained is in the small minority of them who are determined to fulfill their moral obligation, many even spending more quality time with their children than do white nonresidential fathers.[38]

The same can also be said of social fathers from the extended family or local community who sometimes nobly step in when the biological father is absent. After a series of qualitative interviews with black urban middle-school boys raised by single mothers, Leon D. Caldwell and Joseph L. White (2006) concluded that "the rich relationships which boys shared with social fathers fulfilled their fathering needs with emotional and social support, quality time spent together, teaching and instructive talk and guidance about sex and drugs, problem solving, and family values."[39] But the overriding issues must be whether these surrogate role models are readily available and predominantly positive. A number of studies indicate that many black men are willing to become responsible role models for fatherless black boys, but willingness is surely not enough. Potential candidates are sometimes met with insurmountable obstacles. Some may have their own families and lack the time necessary for frequent, consistent visitations with an additional child. Others may be so financially distraught that social fathering is beyond their scope or capacity. And still a few may be constrained by factors as simple as proximity or logistics.

Whatever the case, these explanations may provide some insight into the conclusion drawn by many established social scientists (e.g., sociologist Dr. Orlando Patterson, psychologist Dr. Spencer Holland, and education specialist Dr. Nell Noddings) that there is in fact a vacuum of positive male role models or surrogate fathers in the black community.[40] In addition, says Harvard University sociology professor Orlando Patterson (2006), "Many African-American boys raised by single mothers display an almost exaggerated masculinity in adolescence [because they have] turned to the most aggressive boys … as father substitutes."[41]

Essentially, our black male children are in a blind, desperate search for father figures who will help fill the immeasurable void left by their biological fathers. They seek someone who will teach them how to cope, survive, and perhaps even reach the elusive American dream that is so heavily flaunted in the magazines they read, in the music they listen to, and in the television programs they watch. Because of their wholesale rejection of all things academic, the people that black boys ultimately choose to emulate are usually limited to accessible gang members and drug dealers within their communities and inaccessible professional athletes and famous rappers outside their communities. Choosing the former (gang members and drug dealers) manifests itself in increased aggressive behavior, violent tendencies, and criminality. Choosing the latter (professional athletes and famous rappers) reinforces the delusive and self-defeating notions that academic achievement is an exercise in futility; that delaying gratification is unnecessary; and that fame and fortune are not only easily attainable, but are the antidote for an unassailable lack of self-confidence, uncontrollable feelings of anxiety and frustration, and a deeply rooted fear of racial rejection. As aforementioned, to choose a role model who has succeeded on the basis of education is not an option in the mind of a child who has been socialized to accept the baseless railings of his peers: that pursing intellectual development is "a white thing"; that school is for the weak, the feminine, and the Uncle Toms; and that with or without an education, the black man will always be viewed and treated as just another *nigger*—judged strictly by the color of his skin.

## Expectations of Racial Rejection

The foundation of these beliefs partially emanates from the single mother's unilateral effort to prepare her sons for what she considers a racist America bent on destroying black men. In her attempt to shield and protect her child from the discrimination that she perceives he will one day surely confront, she teaches him to anticipate race-based prejudice and maltreatment. But instead of building within him the strength and resiliency that any mother would desire, she has in effect crippled him with feelings of hatred, fear, and paranoia. Our black boys are being socialized to expect a level of racial rejection that has not existed since the 1960s. Based on a poll conducted by Opinion Research Corporation (2006), although the vast majority of blacks and whites agree that racism still exists in the United States, only 18 percent of whites categorized it as *a serious problem*, while nearly half (49 percent) of blacks categorize it as such.[42] One would be considered naïve and out of touch to contend that prejudice, racism, and discrimination have been completely expunged from our society. On the other hand, one would have to be socially and politically blind to insist that black people still live in a 1960s racist America or that significant progress toward equal opportunity has not been made. Proof of the matter is evidenced by the fact that a black man emerged as president-elect (Senator Barack Obama in 2008) of the United States; this would have been virtually impossible during the lifetime of Dr. Martin Luther King, Jr.

The condition of blacks in the 1920s—the decade that produced our beloved Martin—left a great deal to be desired. Blacks were "kept in their place" by legalized racial discrimination (Jim-Crowism) in the South and economic discrimination in the North. On the heels of the Compromise of 1877 and the subsequent end of Reconstruction, Southern state legislatures, with the help of several key Supreme Court decisions (e.g., *Plessy v. Ferguson* in 1896, *Mississippi v. Williams* in 1898, and *Cumming v. Board of Education* in 1899), quickly found a way to undermine the Fourteenth Amendment, the Civil Rights Acts of 1866 and 1875, and even the Fifteenth Amendment, which was meant to prohibit disenfranchisement of Negroes. In no uncertain terms, Southern blacks in the 1920s were denied their suffrage rights with little legal recourse; they were rigidly segregated in every public accommodation (streetcars, parks, hotels, hospitals, etc.);

and they were in constant danger from the collective violence of white supremacist groups like the re-emergent Ku Klux Klan.[43]

Northern blacks were not much better off during this period. The decline of European immigration and the expansion of war factories during World War I (1914–1918) set the stage for a huge influx of Southern blacks to Northern industrial cities. Northern whites interpreted the expanding black populations as increased competition for housing, jobs, and political power. They responded in kind with uncompromising racial hostility, full-scale discrimination, and extreme methods of exclusion. Thus, Northern blacks in the 1920s found themselves unable to secure adequate employment, debarred from public accommodations, and restricted to the worst and oldest slums.[44] On a national scale, the social and political impotence of Negroes was self-evident. As of 1929, not one black mayor had ever been elected to govern a U.S. city.[45] Likewise, between 1900 and 1930, only two black representatives had served in the U.S. Congress.

By 1973, just five years after the tragic slaying of Dr. King, blacks could boast of forty-eight actively serving mayors (twelve governing relatively large cities)[46] and a total of twenty-one seats in the U.S. House of Representatives since the turn of the century. This drastic change in the American political landscape is undoubtedly reflective of the significant economic and social progress made by black people between 1960 and 1969. During this period, the proportion of blacks below the poverty line fell from 50 percent to 33 percent, while overall black family income rose to 60 percent of white family income (an improvement of 20 percent since 1940).[47] Blacks were increasingly "seen in the offices of banks and big corporations, in the federal civil service, on campuses of leading colleges, as sports stars and television announcers, [and] in officers' clubs, theaters, and tourist haunts."[48] And, not surprisingly, a large black middle class began to emerge, exhibiting a lifestyle comparable to that of the white middle class.[49]

Such enormous gains were symptomatic of the social revolution that began with President Harry S. Truman's integration of the Armed Forces in 1949 and continued with the historic 1954 Supreme Court ruling in *Brown v. Board of Education of Topeka,* which outlawed the "separate but equal" doctrine of *Plessy v. Ferguson* (1896) and required the desegregation of school districts nationwide.[50] In the 1950s, however, Southerners remained indignant and balked at the *Brown* decision—just as they did, and continued to do, in response to the Fifteenth Amendment. By 1957, less than 12 percent of the South's school districts were integrated, and only about 25 percent of eligible Southern blacks were permitted to vote.[51] These realities spurred the second leg of the social revolution, which included the impetus of the civil rights movement (1955–1968) and the passing of the civil rights Acts of 1957, 1960, and 1964, the Voting Rights Act of 1965, and the Fair Housing Act of 1968. But even with the symbolic, legal, and rhetorical evidence of progress, as of 1970, blacks remained subjugated in virtually all American communities. School segregation was maintained in many districts through subtle reorganization. The voting power of blacks was kept to a minimum by gerrymandering voting districts.[52] And, according to a commission of inquiry (1968) set up by President Lyndon B. Johnson, there was still "pervasive discrimination and segregation in employment, education and housing."[53] Even Dr. Martin

Luther King, Jr. (1968), who was the first to acknowledge the triumphs of the period, saw the American "promised land" as a distant place in time, far beyond the 1960s.[54]

Early twenty-first-century America may not prove to be King's promised land, but the chasm between 1968 and 2008 is rods deep and miles wide. The myriad achievements enjoyed by a host of black people in just the last twenty years is clear evidence of the endless opportunities now available to *anyone* who is determined, confident, and prepared. Are there still isolated roadblocks based on race? Any person of good conscience would have to answer in the affirmative. But to then assume that there are impenetrable barriers limiting progress as there were before 1970 is simply belied by the record. As Juan Williams so aptly stated in his book *Enough* (2006), "Racism is no longer [potent] enough to stop most black people from fighting through the static and making their way to a better life."[55] Many ambitious black Americans in recent history would find absolute truth in Williams' statement. Never had there been a sole black owner of a major television production company until Oprah Winfrey formed Harpo Productions in 1986. Never had there been a black quarterback to start in the Super Bowl until Doug Williams earned that honor in 1988. Never had there been a black president of an Ivy League university until Ruth Simmons took the helm of Brown University in 2001. Never had a black politician been elected by the citizens of a state to serve as governor until Douglas Wilder of Virginia and Deval Patrick of Massachusetts changed that fact in 1990 and 2006 respectively. Never had there been a black surgeon general of the United States until Jocelyn Elders was appointed in 1993. Never was a black secretary of state chosen by a sitting president until Colin Powell was selected in 2001, followed by Condoleezza Rice in 2005. And yet despite these and other historic precedents, many well-intentioned black single mothers pass on to their sons the dated and destructive concept of "The Man"—a white enemy waiting to inflict on them some sort of social damage. In other words, our black boys are being groomed to take their place in what John McWhorter (2001) called the *Cult of Victimology*.

According to McWhorter, "Black Americans too often teach one another to conceive of racism not as a scourge on the wane but as an eternal pathology changing only in form and visibility, and always on the verge of getting not better but worse."[56] Blacks have a vested interest in minimizing all signs of racial progress and maintaining their status as victims. They are caught up in an *ideological holding pattern* where the crutch of victimization is passed on like a family totem from one generation to another. In *The Content of Our Character* (1990), Shelby Steele makes the point that black people "*choose* to believe in their inferiority, not to fulfill society's prophesy about them, but for the comforts and rationalizations their racial 'inferiority' affords them. They hold [back] their race to evade individual responsibility."[57] Exaggerating their plight gives them a sense of moral exemption from the social norms that other Americans are obliged to follow. Our black boys have been so seduced by the rhetoric of victimology that any notion to the contrary is simply dismissed as the vitriolic rants of a white racist or a black Uncle Tom. Being taught that racial equality is an oxymoron and that racial rejection is inevitable has instilled in our sons strong feelings of hatred, fear, and paranoia, as well as a blind tolerance for their own failure, lack of effort, and criminality.[58]

## Summary

The family of orientation, as essential as it is to the growth and development of our children, is failing our black boys and sabotaging their futures. As we have shown, the majority of fatherless black males in the United States are born to an economically disadvantaged, poorly educated, never-married teenage mother whose role as the custodial parent has been severely compromised by a lack of paternal resources. They are born into a family structure with a female head who naturally sees herself as the daughter's primary role model and as the son's temporary benefactor; whose educational priorities favor her daughters over her sons; who may even resent the son for the misdeeds of the father; and who, in her attempt to protect her sons from race-based prejudice and maltreatment, teaches them to expect a level of racial rejection that has not existed in over thirty years. Nonetheless, it is the biological father, through his absence and noninvolvement, who has the greatest negative impact on the outcomes of his children. He denies his sons access to their first and most important role model—their own father. He teaches them in absentia that fatherhood is *a joke*, and that "blackness" is synonymous with an uncaring attitude and irresponsible behavior. He leaves them reeling and searching for a definition of manhood that usually manifests itself in over-aggression and extreme machismo. And he makes them feel as if they were fundamentally flawed and not worthy of the paternal love and affection that other children seem to take for granted. Out of these familial circumstances, our black boys tend to develop greater deficiencies in social communication skills, in appropriate self-expression, in delaying gratification, and in their ability to perform and achieve academically.

# 2

# The Influence of the School System

*Treat people as if they were what they*
*ought to be and you help them to become*
*what they are capable of being.*

—Johann Wolfgang von Goethe

Because of the immediate and long-term benefits it offers to its students, and the time and commitment it requires by law, the school system can legitimately be considered a second home to our nation's children. In fact, most school districts provide a laundry list of core services to youth and families as a part of their effort to educate their young patrons. Some of these services include (1) district-wide transportation to and from school; (2) free and reduced-cost breakfast and lunch programs; (3) individual and family counseling; (4) career guidance, training, and placement; (5) referrals to community-based services; (6) after-school recreation; (7) pregnancy prevention programs; and (8) learning support services. As such, the school system offers children much more than a quality education; it makes available to them an unparalleled system of structure and support that could make the difference between ultimate success and ultimate failure.

Without a doubt, the influence of this agency of socialization is superseded only by that of the family of orientation.

However, when it comes to our black boys, even this noble institution (the school system) is riddled with internal deficiencies. First, there is a severe lack of black male teachers to serve as positive role models and to help change the perception of education being "a white, feminine thing." Second, the majority of educators tend to have low academic expectations of their black male students, which leads to differential treatment and a subconscious unwillingness to go beyond the pale for these students. And third, the school system itself seems to be predisposed to categorizing and labeling our black boys in response to shortcomings that might be corrected in more positive ways.

## A Lack of Black Male Teachers

On the first day of school, black male students across the country enter the classroom with their talents and abilities suppressed, using inappropriate behavior and misplaced aggression to mask their inadequacies, already prepared to fail or to do as little as possible to pass. As Beverly Daniel Tatum alluded to in *Can We Talk About Race?* (2007), black students perceive academic achievement as being inextricably connected to *white* behavior. Thus, their rejection of education is really a resistance to "acting white" and an expression of "authentic blackness."[1] Those few who fail to toe the line and dare to achieve and strive for academic success are quickly brought back to reality as they are thoroughly disparaged by their peers. John U. Ogbu (2003), an educational anthropologist who has written extensively on the *acting-white hypothesis*, is very clear about the sacrifices some black students make to avoid social ridicule. Even in affluent suburban neighborhoods, according to Ogbu, capable, intelligent, well-informed black students dumb down their talents and abilities in order to "fit in." These students risk being labeled, teased, and ostracized if they bring books and materials to class, raise their hands to answer questions, do their schoolwork and homework, or get good grades. This *act-your-color* syndrome, says Ogbu, is most pervasive among high school students, but evidence of its effects can be seen as early as middle school.[2]

Does this mean, then, that race is the only undergirding factor in this pandemic of "anti-intellectualism"? Prudence L. Carter (2006) claims, "The explanations for achievement differences are more complex than the acting-white hypothesis can accommodate."[3] She contends that although race is an important factor in understanding black anti-intellectualism, it is certainly not the only factor. Acting white is not just a *racialized* label, according to Carter, but it is also a *feminized* one. In other words, gender roles, sexuality, and race all share in the construction of black male attitudes toward education. For example, as a consequence of their broken families, young black males have adopted a mode of masculinity that is diametrically opposed to the behaviors needed for success in school. They consider behaviors like speaking Standard English, sitting and paying attention in class, and going to class daily as effeminate in nature.

So, because our black boys categorize academic achievement as "acting white" and being feminine, it is not unreasonable to assume that there is a desperate need for more teachers in

America's classrooms who look like them—potential role models who could break down the barriers of race and gender in our nation's school systems. As of now, however, the demographic data does not look very promising. In 2004, the National Center for Educational Statistics (NCES) reported that of the 3 million public school teachers in the United States, approximately 83 percent were white and 8 percent were black. Similarly, 75 percent were female and 25 percent were male. Out of these sobering numbers the most poignant facts emerge. That is, black students constitute about 16 percent of the public school population, while black male teachers constitute only 2.4 percent of the teaching force. There are some schools, says Jawanza Kunjufu (2006), where there is not one black male in the entire building.[4]

For a long time now, and even still, the future of our black boys has been in the hands of white female teachers who mean well, but who cannot be role models to these students, who cannot relate to their experiences, who may even be afraid of them to some degree, and who may expect less from them academically than they do from their other students. This milieu of alienation in our public schools serves only to validate and exacerbate the preexisting black male attitude that academic achievement is indeed for the white and the female. But has this always been our academic reality? Is there any credence to John McWhorter's (2001) contention that between Emancipation and the mid-1960s "blacks were as hungry for education as any American group,"[5] and that black anti-intellectualism was almost a nonissue during this one-hundred-year period?

After freedom was snatched from the jaws of servitude via a bloody civil war, the newly manumitted former slaves sought only refuge, survival, suffrage, and education. For two hundred years these African bondservants languished under the philosophy that "an educated slave is a dangerous slave." At the dawn of freedom, they were determined to take ownership of what was now rightfully theirs. In this effort they had no greater partner than the government-sponsored Freedmen's Bureau, which established and maintained thousands of schools for the education of ex-slaves between 1865 and 1872. But after the Bureau was dissolved, it was blacks themselves who insured that these schools remained operational and that their educational tradition remained intact.[6] As Maldwyn A. Jones concluded in *The Limits of Liberty* (1991), "The black passion for education was unmistakable. Freedmen young and old flocked to the classroom. As Booker T. Washington remarked: 'It was a whole race trying to go to school.'"[7]

At the end of the Civil War, 90 percent of blacks were concentrated in the South, and only about 5 percent of them could read and write. By 1910, through blind effort and sheer determination, 70 percent of blacks were literate. Much like John McWhorter, H. Richard Milner and Tyrone C. Howard (2004) also maintain that this unbridled enthusiasm for academic achievement in the black community did not begin to wane until around the 1960s.[8] Black boys, in particular, displayed severe attitudinal and behavioral changes during this period that were in direct opposition to positive school performance.[9] So, what significant events took place during the turbulent 1960s that could have caused such a dramatic change in the cultural landscape of black America? Why would a whole nation of black boys begin to perceive what may have been their only key to opportunity—being properly educated—as "acting white" and being feminine?

The story begins in 1950 with an unforeseen dilemma: How does the NAACP's Legal Defense Fund (a talented team of attorneys commissioned by the National Association for the Advancement of Colored People to fight for equal citizenship rights) fight the "separate but equal" doctrine of *Plessy v. Ferguson* (1896) with the argument that "separate" is inherently unequal, without debasing and destroying a vital organ of black culture— the black community-based school system? Although the vast inequalities in funding and facilities were undeniable, the intricate, indispensable role that black segregated schools played (along with church and family) in the lives of black children was virtually ignored. Black students, males and females alike, had a deeply rooted hunger for education that was due, in large measure, to the influence of these so-called disadvantaged schools. By 1950, the goal of Thurgood Marshall (the lead counsel of the Legal Defense Fund) and the NAACP was to defeat *Plessy* and mandate nationwide desegregation with a clear argument: that "segregating black children in separate schools, regardless of the quality of those schools, led to an inferior education, [which] violated their right to equal protection of the law guaranteed by the Fourteenth Amendment to the Constitution."[10] As well-meaning as this argument may have been, it was, without question, an unequivocal denigration of a dedicated institution of 140,000 competent, caring black teachers (both men and women) who were embedded in the same communities as their students and who had a vested interest in their outcomes. By definition, therefore, the success of the NAACP would mean the obsolescence of this long-standing black institution and the displacement of thousands of its teachers.

As it turned out, the goal of nationwide desegregation was ultimately achieved after the passing of the Civil Rights Act of 1964. The 1954 Supreme Court decision in *Brown v. Board of Education of Topeka* gave black children the *right* to be educated in white schools. *Brown v. Board of Education II* (1955) provided for the implementation of that right. But almost ten years after *Brown II*, less than 2 percent of black children in the affected school districts actually attended integrated schools. It was not until the federal government was given the authority to deny federal funds to segregated school districts by the Civil Rights Act of 1964 that schools were finally integrated with "all deliberate speed."[11] From this point forward, America's public schools would never be the same. Black children were systematically ripped from the classrooms of a school system that had nurtured and strengthened their communities for almost one hundred years. They were taken from teachers who were like surrogate parents to them—role models and advocates who had only their best interest at heart. But what did these children receive in return for their sacrifice? Most of them were bused miles from their homes only to enter culturally alien environments where they were constantly ridiculed and harassed. They were taught mainly by white female teachers who had no earnest desire to teach them. And ironically, according to Raymond Wolters (1984), although they were now in well-funded, well-equipped schools, their academic performance actually declined, while their behavioral problems became more common.[12]

So, for black students, the mid-1960s marked the beginning of an unprecedented shift away from academic achievement. In one fell swoop, the face of education had dramatically changed for them. As a consequence of *Brown* and the Civil Rights Act of 1964, the community-based, segregated black schools were forced to close, and thousands of black male and female teachers were demoted, fired, or coerced to leave the profession. The magnitude of these closings and job losses had a devastating effect on the black community and on the academic achievement of black students.[13] Of course, black boys seemed to have experienced the greatest degree of alienation as they found themselves completely unable to relate to the new face of education—the white female teacher. It was out of these bleak circumstances that the *acting white and feminine* syndrome was born.

In light of this history and present-day realities, we must ask the obvious question: Would an exclusive environment of all black male teachers help to change the perception that black boys have of education, and hence, improve their overall academic achievement? This age-old question of whether black children need separate schools has been discussed in many forums. But the best answer to date was given by W. E. B. DuBois almost thirty years before anti-intellectualism was even an issue, during a time when segregated schools were the norm. In *Does the Negro Need Separate Schools?* (1935), DuBois implores the concerned not to fall into the trap of pitting segregated schools against mixed schools, because neither is a magic solution. A quality education, according to DuBois, consists of three basic criteria: (1) safe, adequately equipped, well-built facilities; (2) competent, caring, culturally empathetic, well-paid teachers; and (3) a classroom milieu of high expectations, complete acceptance, and social equality.[14] Theoretically, then, children can be educated in *any* school that offers them a quality education based on these criteria. DuBois, however, being a realist, made it clear that as of 1935 (the year his article was published), when institutionalized discrimination was deeply entrenched in American society, if black children did not have separate schools, they would not have been educated.[15]

Can the same be said of black boys today? Has the public school system denied them the essential prerequisites for academic achievement that black male teachers are more prone to provide: equal treatment, cultural acceptance, high expectations, discipline, and role modeling? Beverly Daniel Tatum (2007) contends that this is absolutely the case. Black boys are stifled, says Tatum, by unequal treatment and lowered expectations generated from the old stereotypes that they are stupid, lazy, dangerous, and hypersexual.[16] They are, in effect, languishing in classrooms where their cultural identities are neither recognized nor affirmed.[17] As such, whether in separate or mixed facilities, black boys need black male teachers in the school system as desperately as they need their black fathers at home. It must be understood, however, that this need is less about the race or gender of the teacher (with the exception of role modeling), and more about how the race or gender of the student influences the teacher's perceptions and expectations. Nonetheless, it does logically follow that teachers who share the same race and gender as their students are less likely to be negatively influenced and more likely to have high expectations of them.

## Low Academic Expectations

Is it sheer coincidence that the highest achieving students in the public schools (white females)[18] are represented by the largest portion of the teaching force, or that the lowest achieving students (black males) are represented by the smallest portion? White female teachers certainly bear the heaviest burden in the public school system. The success or failure of more than 65 percent[19] of America's classrooms lies in their hands. They have made significant contributions to our nation's children. But what *identity orientations* does this large block of educators bring to the classroom? And how are our black boys affected by the predominance of these orientations?

Gary R. Howard (1999), a white anthropologist and social psychologist who provides extensive cultural awareness training to schools and universities nationwide, contends that there are three distinct "ways (modalities) of being white." In other words, white female teachers interact with our black boys with one of three *white identity orientations*: either (1) the fundamentalist white identity, (2) the integrationist white identity, or (3) the transformationist white identity.[20] Each of these orientations is profoundly different, according to Howard, in terms of how whites *think* relative to the constructs of "whiteness" and dominance; how whites *feel* relative to racial differences and discussions of racism; and how whites *act* relative to teaching and cross-cultural interactions.[21] He makes it emphatically clear that racial identities and perceptions are not innate characteristics, but that they are part of "a socially and psychologically constructed process." Many whites, says Howard, have been "inculcated with more negative images than positive regarding racial categories, necessitating considerable unlearning and reevaluation in the process of acquiring positive racial attitudes and identity."[22] Ideally, then, the three white identity orientations could represent a process of deliberate self-reflection and growth for white educators. So, how does Howard describe his three modalities of "whiteness"?

Those teachers who are categorized as *fundamentalist whites* tend to be linear thinkers with a single-dimensional understanding of the truth. They believe that white dominance is simply a part of American life, and it should be perpetuated and taken for granted. Many so-called well-intentioned fundamentalist white educators promote a doctrine of "colorblindness" that they presume to be the highest standard of equal treatment. That is, if all students were treated the same and properly assimilated into the primary (white) culture, there would be no need for multicultural education or cultural empathy on the part of teachers. Individuals of this particular point of view do not consider themselves as insensitive or racist, but as strong advocates of what they believe is best for students, especially students of color.

Teachers of the *integrationist* orientation differ from fundamentalist whites in that "[they] acknowledge the existence and legitimacy of diverse approaches to the truth."[23] They even recognize that white dominance has had a negative impact on some racial and ethnic groups. Nonetheless, for integrationist whites, these acknowledgments and concessions are superficial at best. They still maintain subtle feelings of racial superiority and would never entertain the need for a fundamental change in white consciousness. As educators, they are primarily concerned with the compliance and assimilation of their students, although they attempt to respond positively to diversity. And very seldom do they establish close or deeply personal relationship with students of different cultures.

*Transformationist whites*, on the other hand, represent educators who have made a conscious, deliberate effort to dramatically alter their mode of thinking. They have learned to question and challenge tacit assumptions of the truth. They are motivated by a need not only to fully dismantle the remnants of white dominance, but to reach out to those groups that have suffered, historically, under its reign. In their classrooms, transformationist teachers welcome diversity and encourage cross-cultural and cross-racial interactions as they seek to foster "equity, inclusion, and empowerment for all their students."[24]

So, which of these modalities or identity orientations is most represented among the two million white female educators in the public school system? There is little doubt that white female educators of the transformationist orientation are more effective with their black male students than those of the fundamentalist or integrationist orientations. Patricia M. Cooper (2002) even went so far as to say that in many ways these transformationist or independent white teachers have much in common with their effective black counterparts.[25] But while the transformationist identity represents the best of the three modalities, it is also the most difficult to attain. It requires an unrelenting, indefatigable effort by teachers with a singular passion to reach every student, regardless of race, ethnicity, or national origin. These teachers seek remedies for their deficiencies by choosing the path of *most* resistance. They are convinced that if a student does not learn, it is due to the shortcomings of the teacher and nothing else. They are willing to analyze and reconstruct their own subconscious notions of dominance and race in order to become truly effective teachers.

Nevertheless, as Glenn E. Singleton and Curtis Linton alluded to in *Courageous Conversations About Race* (2006), the transformationist white teacher is more of a fluke than a norm. In fact, they claim that the vast majority of white educators are resistant to introspection and are more prone to blaming students of color than themselves for the academic achievement gap between racial groups.[26] Most whites, according to Singleton and Linton, are still bound by the entrenched philosophy that "people of color should be 'integrated into white society and culture' and become 'worthy of acceptance by the white way of life.'"[27] What this means, then, is that our black boys are being taught mainly by white female teachers of the fundamentalist and integrationist orientations whose perceptions of their students are filtered through a prism of white dominance and social privilege. And there can be no gainsaying of the fact that perceptions dictate expectations.

Throughout our nation's history, the black male image has always been painted with a very broad brush dipped in a well of propaganda, lies, and half-truths. Why is it that a black male face is so easily conjured in the minds of most white Americans with a simple mention of words like *stupid, lazy, dangerous,* and *hypersexual?* Why is it that intelligent, hardworking, law-abiding, family-oriented black men are viewed more as exceptions than as representatives of their people? For more than three hundred years now, the descendents of the purloined African have been disparaged and characterized as roving beasts ensconced in criminality and sexual deviance.

Earl Ofari Hutchinson (1996) contends that this perpetual black-male bashing was not without its motivations. Plantation masters of the antebellum South maintained their power and control over a very lucrative industry by painting the black man as a cunning, calculating, subhuman savage who was rescued from idolatry and cannibalism by the institution of slavery.[28] Between the post-Reconstruction period and the mid-twentieth century, the primary goal of white social and political domination was met, first, by convincing Northern and Southern whites that black men ultimately sought to take their jobs, land, political power, and white women; and second, by bombarding whites with pseudo-scientific literature that "proved" that the black male was, by nature, a mentally defective, violent, sex-crazed degenerate who deserved no special rights or privileges.[29] Black-male bashing was also used during the Ronald Reagan–George Bush–Newt Gingrich years (defining black men as derelict and lazy) to justify the rolling back of civil rights and the slashing of social programs.[30] It is this unflattering history that has had the greatest influence on white perceptions of black males. But are the primary educators of our black boys—fundamentalist and integrationist white female teachers—led and guided, either consciously or subconsciously, by these perceptions? The only available litmus test is whether these teachers have high or low expectations of their black male students.

In a recent article, Julie Landsman (2004), a white professor of urban and multicultural education and a former educator in the Minneapolis public school system, shared two anecdotal experiences that one would hope were uncommon, isolated circumstances. But the sad truth is, in accordance with a large body of research,[31] they are neither uncommon nor isolated. In the first story, Landsman recalls teaching an intelligent young white woman in a multicultural education course at an academically rigorous college in Northfield, Minnesota. As a junior in the education department at that time, this exceptional student would become a fully licensed teacher after only one additional year of schooling; and yet, in a final paper for Landsman's class, she wrote the following revealing statement: "It is good I took this class from you, because before I took it, I thought all black people were stupid because they let themselves be slaves."[32] In the second story, black students in an advanced placement class in a St. Paul, Minnesota high school complained that their very well-meaning teacher (a white woman) consistently directed complex or critical thinking questions to her white students and reserved the easy questions that "anyone could answer" for her black and Latino students. "When confronted with this situation, the teacher was stunned. She realized it was true and admitted, 'I just assumed you didn't know the answers, and I didn't want to embarrass you.'"[33]

The most perplexing factor about these two stories presented by Landsman is that there is absolutely no evidence of overt racism. In many cases, teachers who harbor no ill will and have the best of intentions perpetuate low expectations. Even white teachers with "hearts of gold" have been socialized to accept the notion that black people are a *problem people*, rather than fellow American citizens with problems.[34] By definition, the latter condition is solvable, while the former condition is not. So, whether America's public schools are predominated by the *missionary* teacher who proselytizes on behalf of her own culture as a way of saving the culturally deprived, by the *liberal* teacher who overlooks bad behaviors, accepts inferior work, and gives unearned grades, or by the *insensitive* teacher who makes no attempt to understand the culture of others,[35] low academic expectations of black male students remain a common thread.[36]

Be that as it may, some underestimate the impact of teacher expectations on student performance. A classic study conducted in the 1960s by a prominent social psychologist and a veteran elementary school principal, Robert Rosenthal and Lenore Jacobson (1968) respectively, is often cited as an authoritative demonstration of the power of expectations. Increasingly concerned about the high rates of failure among lower class and minority children, Rosenthal and Jacobson sought to determine whether the theory of *self-fulfilling prophecy* was at work in the classroom.

They began their study by administering a standardized, nonverbal IQ test to a large group of elementary school students at the very beginning of the school year, leading teachers to believe that this test not only determined intelligence quotients (IQs), but that it also predicted intellectual *blooming* or *spurting*. Teachers were informed directly of the particular students entering their classrooms who were expected to *flourish* during the coming year, despite their current abilities. In other words, any differences between these children and the rest of the class existed only in the minds of the teachers. And if Rosenthal and Jacobson's assumptions were correct, those students who were labeled as *special* or *more prone to excel* would receive more attention, preferential treatment, and constant pressure to succeed, resulting in better performance and higher achievement. At the end of the school year, when all of the children were retested using the same nonverbal measure, Rosenthal and Jacobson's assumptions were confirmed. Those children who were initially identified as bloomers had exceeded levels well beyond the children who lacked the *expectancy advantage*.

In short, based on this historic experiment, there is a strong correlation between teacher expectations and student performance.[37] Might this at least partially explain why our black boys lag so far behind all other social groups in grade point averages, in standardized test scores, in graduation rates, and in college attendance?[38] Might we begin to gain some insight as to why black male students are overrepresented in special education programs and disproportionately categorized as mentally deficient or learning disabled?

## Predisposed to Categorizing Black Boys

In a climate of low expectations where school officials are predisposed to categorizing and labeling black boys, noble creations like special education programs have become what they were never meant to be. Some have called special education, in particular, a new, more insidious form of segregation[39] "covered up by certain niceties of complexity." It has become, for most schools, *the* incontrovertible answer for what are considered the *innate* shortcomings of black male students. Special education programs today are essentially dumping grounds for the hyperactive, the impulsive, the inattentive, the stubborn, the irritable, and the aggressive—all personality traits that could very well plague a child who feels alienated, invalidated, and mistreated. According to the National Center for Educational Statistics (2008) there are approximately 50 million students (grades K–12) enrolled in America's public school system. Of these students, 6 million have been placed in special education programs, and nearly half (2.9 million) were placed as a consequence of being categorized as learning disabled.[40] Because teachers generate 80 percent of referrals, our black boys (the victims of low expectations) are much more likely than other groups to be tested and labeled as learning disabled and recommended for special education. In fact, 1 in every 50 black male students currently receive LD-related special education services, compared to 1 in 150 white males, 1 in 200 black females, and 1 in 300 white females. Black boys represent only 8 percent of the public school population, but fully 25 percent of special education students.[41] These disparities, in and of themselves, bring into question the validity of the entire special education process, "from the quality of instruction prior to referral, to the decision to refer; and from the assessment and placement of the student in a special education program, to the quality of instruction that occurs in that program."[42] But has special education always been so suspect?

Special or *specialized* education actually began as a very noble idea with the best of intentions. Its original purpose, as promoted by early nineteenth century reformers like Jean-Marc-Gaspard Itard, Thomas Hopkins Gallaudet, and Dorothea Dix, was to ameliorate the often neglectful and abusive treatment of individuals with apparent disabilities. During much of the 1800s, many of the blind, the deaf, the mentally retarded, and the physically handicapped were confined in jails, almshouses, residential facilities, and asylums without decent food, clothing, personal hygiene, exercise, or education. By the end of the nineteenth century, however, the tide had begun to change dramatically for the better. State governments, nationwide, established juvenile courts and social welfare programs that provided foster home placement services for children and adolescents in need. Many states also passed laws mandating compulsory education (existing in all states by 1918), which, along with the grassroots efforts of burgeoning parent advocacy groups, helped lay the foundation for the introduction of special classes within regular public schools for children with apparent disabilities.

Throughout the first half of the twentieth century, parent advocacy groups, such as the American Association on Mental Deficiency (1876), the Council for Exceptional Children (1922), and the National Association for Retarded Citizens (1950), continued to secure local ordinances that would further protect and serve individuals with special needs. By the late 1950s, the permanent establishment of special education in the public school system was well under way, absent a federal mandate. The *Education for All Handicapped Children Act* (Public Law 94-142), signed into law by President Gerald Ford on November 29, 1975, provided that mandate.

Nonetheless, even after the passage of PL 94-142, *special* was still intended to refer to "a very small percentage of children with severe handicaps who might be left uneducated because their parents did not have enough money for private tutors or schools."[43] But because school districts had a strong financial incentive (guaranteed federal funding) to expand the meaning of *special*, and a readily exploitable population of students (black boys), special education has definitely become what it was never meant to be—a "dumping ground" for the intolerable via questionable methods of assessment.

With the obvious exception of assessing and placing those who are visually and hearing impaired, severely mentally retarded, and physically handicapped, the *subjective* evaluation process used to determine special education eligibility is naturally exposed to error, bias, and outright corruption. At the very least, evidence of bias is reflected in the fact that black boys are three to six times more likely than other students to receive LD-related special education services.

So, who is an LD child, and how is he diagnosed as such? Charles is a respectful, obedient child at home, but he has severe disciplinary problems at school. He has consistently earned above-average standardized test scores and has done well throughout elementary and middle school. But beginning in ninth grade, his grades plummeted, and he began to display aggressive and disruptive behaviors. When Charles is in class, between truancies and suspensions, he instigates his peers and does very little work. He complains to his mother that his classes are boring and his teachers don't respect him. In Charles' case, his in-class performance (behavioral and academic) is directly connected to his perceived relationships with his teachers. Charles is an LD child.

John is also a very bright child, who writes poetry and short stories and delights in drawing original cartoons. He even has the uncanny ability to memorize dozens of lines of rap in one sitting, but in the classroom, he shuts down. He refuses to follow instructions and either puts his head down or engages in his own talents. Some teachers have sent John to the office for insubordination, whereas others have simply ignored his behavior and allowed him to *do his own thing*. With the exception of certain fine arts classes, he has received very few passing grades. John is also an LD child. But even with their apparent difficulties, how could two children with such promising backgrounds, talents, and abilities be categorized as learning disabled and placed in special education programs?

The answer is in the evaluation process. Candidates are first given an IQ test as a screening for possible retardation. They are then given a thorough medical exam to insure that their in-class behavior is not related to unknown physical problems. The final part of the process usually consists of vision and hearing assessments. If none of these tests produce a substantive explanation for their poor academic performance, candidates are simply labeled, almost willy-nilly, as *learning disabled*. As many researchers have noted, "The only thing all LD kids have in common is low achievement in class."[44]

Essentially, the school system itself, showing no concern for the quality of teaching prior to referral or for the unique talents and abilities of the many children being evaluated and labeled, has become a pusher and promoter of special education—which might explain why "most schools have a declining general population but an increasing special education population."[45] And what exactly is the school system pushing and promoting? The standard image perpetuated by school officials is one where special education represents a competent delivery of specialized services by a ready team of diverse, experienced, well-trained professional educators who are certified to teach disabled, disturbed, and deficient children. Nothing could be further from the truth. In fact, special education teachers are even less ethnically diverse than teachers in general education classrooms,[46] and almost one-third of them are unqualified and teaching in schools where black students predominate.[47]

The state of special education has changed very little since the *Education for All Handicapped Children Act* was passed in 1975. For more than thirty years now, special education programs have had to navigate the difficult terrain between maintaining professional standards and mitigating persistent teacher short-ages, leading, in most cases, to a sacrifice of quality control and the subsequent academic neglect of participating students. So, in no uncertain terms, our black boys are being targeted, branded, and herded into a program that stigmatizes them, that is too ill equipped and understaffed to properly serve them, and that is not conducive to positive outcomes.

The National Center for Education Statistics reports that in 2006 only 57 percent of students with disabilities graduated high school with a *regular* or standard diploma; and in fourteen states, the number was less than 50 percent. What this means is that too many of these students are either dropping out of high school (25 percent of all special education students and 30 percent of LD students)[48] or are receiving a special education diploma or certificate of attendance.

The real travesty here is that those students who graduate with a special education diploma or a certificate of attendance are not much better off than those who have dropped out. Most colleges and universities will not accept them, and most employers will not hire them.[49] Their future employment, income, and security hang in the balance. But to make matters worse, the National

Education Association (the largest teacher organization and labor union in the United States), in its gracious attempt to put regular diplomas in the hands of more special education students, has established a proposal that would actually taint the validity of regular diplomas, especially those earned by the 57 percent of special needs students who struggled so hard to complete the standard requirements. The NEA proposes that states should be required to make the regular or standard diploma more accessible to students with disabilities by allowing them (1) to earn fewer credits to graduate, (2) to meet lower performance criteria, (3) to take more time to complete courses and meet academic standards, (4) to obtain an exemption from the high school exit exam, and (5) to compile a competency portfolio in lieu of taking required state tests.[50] As aforementioned, these proposed accommodations would only serve to threaten the legitimacy of the regular diploma, making the large pool of unmarketable special education students even larger, and their futures that much bleaker.

## Summary

The public school system has an awesome responsibility and bears the heaviest of burdens. It has been commissioned to successfully educate our nation's children, regardless of race, ethnicity, gender, national origin, or disability. It has been charged with the unparalleled task of preparing young minds for an uncertain future. And in that task, it has had a throng of notable successes. The public school system (along with the family of orientation) is the cornerstone of American society, and it effectively serves millions of children and families. But 8 percent of its population has been left in the lurch. Our black boys are treated as pariahs in an institution that preaches equality, inclusion, and mutual respect. They are taught by their white female teachers, through reaction and response, that their dialect, attitudes, and clothing styles are culturally illegitimate and are actually signs of rebellion and anti-intellectualism. They have been made to feel inadequate, inferior, and self-conscious about their own "blackness" through a constant barrage of low expectations. They are prematurely labeled as "unmanageable" and hastily recommended for special education with the slightest display of hyperactivity, inattentiveness, stubbornness, irritability, or aggressiveness. They are much more likely than any other group to be categorized as *learning disabled* and receive LD-related special education services, to be permanently separated from general education classrooms, and to drop out of school and earn no equivalency diploma. These poignant facts, along with the obvious lack of black male teachers, go a long way toward explaining why our black boys continue to write off academic achievement as *a white, feminine thing*, and why they pursue unrealistic nonacademic goals, like professional sports and entertainment. The school system, like the family of orientation, has been severely negligent in its duty to properly socialize our black boys, leaving them exposed to the exacerbating influences of their peers and the mass media.

# 3

# The Influence of the Peer Group

*If you succeed in life, the credit ultimately
belongs to you. If you fail in life, the
blame ultimately belongs to you.*

—Reginald E. Hicks

Unlike the family of orientation, the school system, and the mass
media, the child's peer group is organized and operated strictly
by children, usually of similar ages and interests. It is, uniquely,
the only nonadult agency of socialization, and it is vital to human
growth and development. Through peer group interactions,
children learn (1) to cooperate, compete, and defend themselves;
(2) to establish friendships, date, and deal with conflict; (3)
to make their own decisions and engage in activities that
involve self-expression; and, generally, (4) to explore the world
independent of parental supervision. The influence of peers is
clearly evident in early childhood, but *peer pressure* reaches its
peak during adolescence—the period of life from puberty to
maturity. It is within this stage of development (between the ages
of twelve and seventeen) that "fitting in" becomes paramount
to children. Many will abandon values instilled by the family

or even sacrifice their own good judgment to satisfy their need for acceptance and stave off the undesirable alternative: rejection, ridicule, and debasement. The black male peer group is especially damaging to our black boys because its members display a nearly homogeneous negative identity, as the majority of them have been jilted and ill-served by the family and the school system. They express themselves by reinforcing black stereotypes, glorifying prison life, and embracing the word *nigger*. They continue the cycle of personal destruction and failure by exacerbating an already bungled socialization process.

## Reinforcing Black Stereotypes

The facts speak for themselves. Beverly Daniel Tatum (2007) is absolutely correct in her assertion that whites tend to have stereotypical perceptions of black males as being stupid, lazy, dangerous, and hypersexual. She is also correct that these perceptions are not necessarily products of overt racism or extreme prejudice.[1] Some may even go so far as to say that prejudice and racism (both defined as unfair generalizations rooted in *unsupported* preconceptions) are completely inadequate explanations for racial stereotypes that seem to be based less on non-experiential, preconceived notions and more on cumulative observations, interactions, and statistics.

Are black males stupid? They are overrepresented in special education programs and underrepresented in honors, AP (Advanced Placement), and IB (International Baccalaureate) courses.[2] They have the lowest GPAs, standardized test scores, and graduation rates in high school and in college.[3] And they compose only 2.5 percent of business owners, 2.5 percent of scientists, and 2 percent of PhDs.[4] Are black males lazy? As adolescents, they tend to reject hard academic work while clinging to the unrealistic dream of easy riches through drug dealing, professional sports, or entertainment.[5] And as adults, the majority of them neglect their fundamental duties as fathers, providers, and protectors.[6] Are black males dangerous? Although they represent only 13 percent of the country's total population, they commit 51 percent of all murders, 32 percent of forcible rapes, 56 percent of robberies, and 34 percent of aggravated assaults.[7] Are black males hypersexual? They have more children out of wedlock per capita than their white and Asian counterparts combined.[8] And the STD rate (including HIV and AIDS) in the black community, itself, is the highest in the nation.[9] So, despite the many possible intervening variables that might explain some of these disparities, for most whites, the evidence is clear, and their perceptions are justified. From their perspective, black males *are* stupid, lazy, dangerous, and hypersexual. And the sad truth is our black boys do absolutely nothing to counter this perspective. In fact, they legitimize it by perpetuating these very same stereotypes within their peer group. They "act out" these expected behaviors as a part of their collective identity and as an expression of "authentic blackness."

In *The Envy of the World* (2002), Ellis Cose recalls his own struggle with identity and self-image in a poor Chicago school district in the 1960s: "Our stupidity [and laziness] was deemed by many of our teachers to be a natural and immutable condition, where the purpose of education therefore was not to enlighten but to help us get through the day."[10] There is no doubt that Cose attended America's public schools at a time when racial stereotypes were usually a direct outgrowth of culturally entrenched racist beliefs filtered through a prism of white dominance and social privilege. But in 2008, although still tinged by a belief in white dominance and privilege, white teachers are much more within their rights to argue that their perceptions of black male students are informed more by what these students present to them on a daily basis than by prejudice or racism. Even John U. Ogbu (2004) contends, "discrimination in society and school, though significant, is not enough to explain why there are differences in school performance among minority groups."[11] He, therefore, offers an alternative explanation. According to Ogbu, the black male peer group, being composed almost exclusively of members who have an *oppositional collective identity* (an identity that is diametrically opposed to white cultural frames of reference), views exhibitions of intelligence and academic conscientiousness among "brothers" as an affront to "authentic blackness" and tantamount to *wanting to be white*. Our black boys, therefore, *act stupid and lazy in the classroom to gain what every adolescent needs*—acceptance by their peers.[12]

But what price are they actually paying for that acceptance? No other peer group is so negative in its outlook and so damaging to its members. No other peer group requires so much sacrifice (e.g., the potential sacrifice of future opportunities) for so little return. It is true that the psyche of our black boys is, to a large degree, the product of the family and the school system; but we must not forget—*choice* is still a factor. The black male peer group has, by choice, become a key contributor to the many statistics that are so injurious to the black male image. It has, by choice, embraced academic failure and repudiated academic success. So, when our black boys are labeled as stupid and lazy because only 48 percent of them graduate high school with a regular diploma (35 percent graduate with a special education diploma or certificate of attendance) and more than 17 percent of them drop out altogether,[13] the black male peer group must shoulder at least part of the responsibility.

It must also share the blame when black males are categorized as overly aggressive and potentially dangerous, likened to violent beasts roaming an urban savanna waiting for any opportunity to display their predatory mentality. This age-old stereotypical image was certainly not created by the black male peer group, but it has been resuscitated, nurtured, and strengthened by it. The *gangsta* profile—boisterous, jive-talking adolescents sporting baggy pants, wife-beaters, and gold teeth—adopted by our black boys as a badge of honor, has become so engrained in the American mindset as a symbol of danger that it serves as a warning not only to whites, but also to other blacks. For example,

> Jesse Jackson said one time that he was walking down the street in the middle of the night [in] Washington, D.C., and he heard footsteps coming across the street, and when he looked around he saw three men coming at him fast. When he saw that they were white, he said that he was relieved.[14]

What this tells us is that there is a general awareness among both blacks and whites that they are four times more likely to be assaulted, two times more likely to be raped, five times more likely to be robbed, and two times more likely to be murdered by a black youth than by a white youth.[15] The statistics are clear. A stereotype that has been reinforced, historically, by propaganda, lies, and half-truths is now reinforced primarily by the delinquent activities of the black male peer group itself.

This unflattering reality is, of course, compounded when peer group members are affiliated with the ultraviolent gang counterculture. As diverse as gangs may be demographically, they all seem to share the same basic precepts: violence, delinquency, and law breaking. According to the *Encyclopedia of Educational Psychology* (2008), "Law-breaking activities enhance the gang's credibility, create fear in the community, and may provide an ongoing source of income for the gang and its members."[16] Our black boys, propelled by fatherlessness and weak family ties, gravitate toward this so-called "family of brothers" to their own detriment and to the detriment of their peer group. In other words, without paternal support and guidance, they almost always turn to peers who have a gang-compatible mentality wherein their manhood is defined not only by an exaggerated masculinity (*fear or be feared*), but also by an untoward hypersexuality.

*The American Heritage Dictionary* defines *hypersexual* as, "Being excessively interested or involved in sexual activity."[17] But the sexual stereotypes pertaining to black males are much more complex than this definition implies. In the minds of white Americans, the mere mention of *black sexuality* conjures up a very specific set of responses: fear, disapprobation, disdain, and disgust. Cornel West (2001), a black studies professor at Princeton University, explains that these visceral responses are fueled by "the dominant myths [that] draw black women and men either as threatening creatures who have the potential for sexual power over whites, or as harmless, desexed underlings of a white culture."[18] Essentially, what West is saying is that white responses to black sexuality are based on the belief that "sexual normalcy" in the black community is virtually nonexistent. And our pants-sagging, crotch-holding, young black males are poster boys of that belief. Through their own public displays they have become symbols of sexual deviance. They can even be categorized as co-conspirators (along with black girls) in creating an STD rate that is unparalleled in the United States. At the 2008 National STD Prevention Conference, the Centers for Disease Control and Prevention (CDC) reported that STDs are more prevalent among black girls than among any other female adolescent group; 48 percent of black teenage girls were found to have one or more common STDs, compared to 20 percent of whites and 20 percent of Hispanics.[19] Even more incriminating are the STD rates of black male and female teens combined. Of all adolescents nationwide, blacks (males and females) represent 75 percent of reported gonorrhea cases, 54 percent of reported chlamydia cases, 71 percent of reported syphilis cases, and 50 percent of new AIDS cases.[20] These sobering statistics inform us that our black boys are minimizing their own humanity and limiting their own potential by reinforcing the old stereotype that they are simply walking phalluses mindlessly fixated on the next conquest.

So, as damaging and destructive as race-based stereotypes have been to black people, historically, why would the black male peer group choose to use these very same stereotypes—which were created, perpetuated, and wielded by white racists—to define its "blackness"? What lucid people would take a weapon from a defeated enemy and destroy themselves with it? As irrational as it sounds, our black boys act stupid, lazy, dangerous, and hypersexual not just as a consequence of fatherlessness or as a part of their resistance to "acting white," but, ironically, as a way of establishing their reputation and maintaining a certain *coolness* in the eyes of their peers. They are constantly measured and judged by the ubiquitous, immutable, stereotypical image of *the young hustler chillin' in the cut* (stupid and lazy), *hittin' them skins* (hypersexual), *and layin' a nigga out at the drop of a hat* (dangerous). This image, for black boys, is the epitome of cool, and the closer one comes to exemplifying this standard, the more respect and admiration one receives from the peer group. As such, to be cool (to model black stereotypes) is to invest in an identity that is both a benefit and a hindrance to its host. On the one hand, "cool" offers acceptance, support, popularity, confidence, and prestige to black males. On the other hand, "cool" requires of them a sacrifice that is sometimes measured in blood.

In *Cool Pose* (1992), Richard Majors and Janet Mancini Billson speculate that cool behavior helps to explain why black boys drop out of school and are suspended more often than white children; why they are more deeply involved in criminal and delinquent activities; why they die earlier and faster than white males from suicide, homicide, accidents, and stress-related illnesses; and why they have more volatile relationships with women.[21] "Cool" is a tough taskmaster that demands unwavering commitment and inordinate sacrifice. It conditions the mind to believe that right is wrong and that wrong is right, that manhood can be achieved by reinforcing black stereotypes, that the word *nigger* should be used as a term of endearment, and that unrepentant convicts should be held up as role models.

## Glorifying Prison Life

With the strong hand of "cool" as their guide, our black boys have come to view even incarceration as a sort of ultimate bar mitzvah for "brothers," making convicted criminals one of their primary reference groups. And what is the profile of the average black male inmate? He is a violent repeat offender with gang affiliations.[22] He is a high school dropout with no diploma or GED.[23] He has several children by different women that he may not claim and cannot support because of his incarceration.[24] And he will spend at least fifteen years of his life (based on typical sentences for violent crimes and the recidivism rate for blacks) as property of the state.[25] This profile, for our black boys, is descriptive of a level of masculinity and prowess that they one day hope to achieve. They have, in a sense, transformed the socially intolerable into the revered and the respected. The professional criminal, who defines himself by his own deviance, has become *the* symbol of manhood for the black male peer group.

That is not to say, however, that young black males would *verbally* express a yearning for imprisonment, because surely they would not. But it is to say that actions speak louder than words, and that their obsession with prison life permeates every aspect of their existence. They carry themselves as if they were led by the nose toward the prison doors. They are stuck in a state of psychosis with like-minded peers and boisterous neighborhood ex-cons as their only counsel. Apparently, the words of Stanley Tookie Williams (co-founder of the Crips, put to death by the state of California in 2005) have fallen on deaf ears: "Prison is no friend of mine. Its objective is to torment my body ... and damage my mind ... I warn black men and women everywhere:

beware of these tombs for the living called prison."[26] From their clothing styles, to the music and movies that they enjoy, our black boys have shown that they are conspicuous consumers of their own glamorized vision of prison life.

This may explain why four million of our children from coast to coast participate in a so-called fashion trend that requires the sagging of one's trousers beyond the point of decency and decorum. No other clothing style has become so identified with black culture or has been so long-standing in the black community. The zoot suit, born out of the big-band-swing era of the 1930s and 1940s, was popularized by blacks, Hispanics, Italian Americans, and Filipino Americans and lasted no longer than twenty years.[27] Bell-bottoms were adopted from the U.S. Navy by the hippie counterculture movement of the 1960s and had an even shorter life span of about eleven years.[28] "Pants-sagging"—allowing one's pants to hang below the buttocks, completely exposing one's underwear—however, has had a hold on our black boys for *more* than twenty years, and its grip seems to be strengthening rather than weakening.[29]

But how could such a clothing style or fashion trend, albeit indecent, be reflective of a glorification of prison life? First and foremost, the concept of sagging pants as an acceptable mode of dress is directly derivative of a prison policy that was emulated and diffused by hip-hop entertainers of the 1980s.[30] That is, beginning in the 1970s, in an effort to reduce inmate access to instruments that could be used as weapons or suicide devices, it became common practice (although not always mandated) to prohibit the wearing of belts in correctional facilities, making loose-fitting, hanging trousers a standard part of the prison milieu.[31] Despite the circumstances of its origin, however, pants-sagging cannot be categorized as just another fashion trend or passing fad rooted in obscurity. In fact, *because* of its origin, pants-sagging has become a strong universal symbol of a peer group enamored by its own fantasy of life behind bars.

Our young black males are so zealous in their identification with prison life that they have even developed an appetite for a genre of music (*gangsta rap*) that is essentially a propaganda tool for the criminal-minded. With its abrasive, law-flouting, misogynistic lyrics, gangsta rap, the dominant form of black urban cultural expression,[32] offers nothing more than unjustified hatred, violence, and criminality set to a hip-hop beat. And yet, from Grandmaster Flash ("The Message"), KRS-One ("9mm Goes Bang"), and Ice-T ("Cop Killer") in the 1980s and 1990s, to The Game ("Hate It or Love It"), T.I. ("What You Know"), and Lil Wayne ("Lollipop") in the new millennium, gangsta rappers have made their fortunes from the blind patronage of our children.[33] Our black boys have such a deep admiration for inmates and ex-cons that the outlaw-touting words of gangsta rappers have become like gospel to them—especially since many of these artists have served time in prison themselves.[34] As such, the black male peer group, bolstered by its chosen music, maintains one consistent public persona shared by its members: loud, impudent, and deviant.

As a case in point, John McWhorter (2003) recalls his own recent observation of a group of young "brothers" (each about fourteen years of age) sitting at a table in a black-owned KFC restaurant in Harlem, New York, being deliberately disruptive, cantankerous, and disrespectful to other KFC customers (most of whom were black) and to the manager, who gave them several warnings before eventually asking them to leave the establishment. The peculiar part of the story began when the boys finally made their way out of the restaurant at the behest of security. Before leaving the property, they circled the business several times in a taunting fashion and, according to McWhorter, "Every so often, one or another of them would break into cocky, expletive-laden rap lyrics, accompanied by the angular, bellicose gestures typical of rap performance."[35] Of course, as commonplace as these types of stories may be, they are by no means proof of causation between rap music and delinquent behavior.[36] But they do bring into question the mindset of young black males who are so fixated on celebrating criminality that they gravitate toward a style of music that does just that—a style of music that has become so ingrained in their consciousness that it seeps out at any time, for any reason. Some may characterize this fixation as *anticipatory socialization* (the voluntary preparation for some future status), where, in this case, those who have an affinity for prison life develop an attraction for those things that are in some way reflective of prison (or criminal) life, such as gangster music, gangster clothing styles (sagging pants), and gangster-oriented movies.

The movie *Scarface* (1983), for example, one of the most popular films among gangsta rappers, has become a cult classic to our black boys. This remake (written by Oliver Stone and directed by Brian De Palma) of Howard Hawks' and Ben Hecht's 1932 film of the same name chronicles the rise and fall of the infamous main character, Tony Montana, as he gets caught up in the all-too-real cocaine boom of the 1980s. Through his own ingenuity, ruthlessness, and greed, the fictional Montana (a character based loosely on the real-life Alphonse Gabriel "Al" Capone) transformed himself from a poor Cuban refugee working at a food stand, to a multimillionaire crime boss in Miami's drug underworld. He ruled his lucrative empire with a strong, steady hand until he broke the cardinal commandment of all drug dealers: never use your own product. His eventual cocaine addiction led to chronic paranoia, severe lapses in judgment, and a continuing cycle of personal destruction that resulted in his ultimate assassination.

Critics have called *Scarface* one of the most objectionable and irredeemable films of its time; nothing less than a collage of blood, violence, and cruelty.[37] It was even, initially, given an X rating for its violent content.[38] And it is this kind of film that our black boys crave, and that their surrogate mentors—gangsta rappers—are obsessed with. Sean "P. Diddy" Combs claims to have viewed *Scarface* more than sixty times because of the "lessons" it teaches.[39] Fat Joe proudly displays a tattoo of Tony Montana on his arm and refers to the character as a "true warrior."[40] Snoop Dog calls the film, "One of the most important movies of all time."[41] The rapper Scarface was so inspired by the film that he took its title as his stage name.[42] And there are dozens upon dozens of *Scarface* references in songs recorded by just about every prominent rap musician.[43]

How can the black male peer group resist the negative leanings of these powerful cultural icons, whose predominance and influence rival the most insidious of cults? Why should there be any surprise when our black boys choose gangs and guns over life and liberty? Their fixation on gangster clothing styles, gangsta rap, and gangster-oriented films may desensitize their minds to criminality as they express their admiration for prison life, but when they participate in street gangs, they *participate* in criminality and have a direct affiliation with prison life—via prison gangs.

Prison gangs are nothing new in the United States. They have been an integral part of the prison experience for nearly seventy years, just as street gangs have plagued our cities for more than two hundred years.[44] Prison gangs were originally created in the 1940s and early 1950s in California, Texas, and Illinois correctional facilities by incarcerated Irish, Jewish, and Italian mob leaders. They used these stealthy organizations as a way of monitoring and controlling the behavior of their incarcerated members and as a form of protection against predatory inmates. Sociologists have argued that these white "con bosses" could be persuaded to promote the administration's basic aims in a tandem effort to prevent major disturbances within the prison system. Beginning in the 1960s, however, these old con bosses were gradually replaced by a younger, more aggressive, more politicized breed of convict chieftain who had no interest in cooperating with prison officials.[45] These new *indiscreetly* violent inmate leaders represented relatively large factions that were predominantly black and Hispanic. For example, as the 1950s brought more street gang violence and the use of firearms among gangs nationwide, Mexican-American street gang members (among others) in East Los Angeles began to go to prison in much larger numbers, leading to the formation, in 1957, of what is now considered the oldest and most powerful of the traditional prison gangs, the Mexican Mafia (also known as EME). In direct opposition to this distinctly urban group, the culturally and socially dissimilar rural Mexican-Americans founded La Nuestra Familia (1968) in California's Soledad State Prison as a way of protecting themselves from the Mexican Mafia. This Hispanic blood feud was, and remains, as pernicious as the ongoing pitched battles between the Black Guerrilla Family and the white supremacist prison gang, the Aryan Brotherhood. The Black Guerrilla Family (BGF), created at California's San Quentin State Prison in 1966 (just one year before the creation of Aryan Brotherhood) as a protective haven for black inmates, is the most politically oriented of the major prison gangs. It was established by former Black Panther member George L. Jackson as a Marxist/Maoist/Leninist revolutionary organization with three central goals: (1) to eradicate racism, (2) to maintain the struggle for dignity in prison, and (3) to overthrow the United States government.[46] Today, the Black Guerrilla Family has strong affiliations with many black prison and street gangs, including the nationally recognized Bloods and Crips.

The Crips and Bloods (both based in Los Angeles) have been bitter rivals since their creation in the late 1960s and early 1970s, respectively. Their names and reputations are known in almost every corner of the North American continent, and their presence has been reported in at least 32 states and 113 cities throughout the U.S.[47] They are known for their involvement in robbery, burglary, homicide, and especially in the trafficking of crack cocaine. Their drug dealings have spread to cities like Seattle, Portland, Denver, Kansas City, Des Moines, and even Honolulu and Anchorage.[48] The street and prison branches of the Bloods and the Crips remain powerful, active organizations from coast to coast,[49] and along with other prominent black gangs like the Vice Lord Nation, the Black Gangster Disciples, the Folk Nation, the People Nation, and the Black P. Stones, they are drawing our black boys into their ranks like a moth to a flame. According to the 2007 National Youth Gang Survey Analysis, of the approximately 760,000 gang members that are reported as being active in 2,900 jurisdictions nationwide, 48 percent are Hispanic, 36 percent are black, 9 percent are white, and 7 percent are Asian and others.[50] Although juveniles represent only about one-third of the 36 percent of active black "gangbangers,"[51] all of the outward signs indicate that a large sector of young black males are waiting with bated breath to take their rightful place. And they are finding, all too often, that their rightful place is beside their "brothers" in the streets, in gangs, and in prison. As they might proudly say to their critics, "These are 'my niggas'."

## Embracing the Word *Nigger*

So, our black boys have found a home in a peer group that perpetuates black stereotypes, that glorifies criminality and prison life, and that "affectionately" refers to its comrades-in-arms as *niggas*. Perhaps it is fitting that a damaging and destructive mindset is accompanied by an equally damaging and destructive label. To use the word *nigger*, in any form, is to promote, at the very least, remnants of its original intent. Black Americans have had to endure many labels since the first West Africans were brought to the shores of the New World in chains, but no label is as vile as *nigger*. For example, according to the *American Heritage Book of English Usage* (1996), *black* and its semantic twin *negro* (generally spelled lowercase) were used as common labels for

Africans or persons of African descent at least since the middle of the sixteenth century. Hence, from American colonial times up until the Civil War, black slaves and free men alike were usually referred to as either *black*, *negro*, *African*, or *nigger*.

After emancipation, black Americans swiftly rejected all of these labels as part of the language of slavery (they considered *African* inappropriate because they were so many generations removed from the continent) and instead preferred *colored* as a more respectful alternative. For more than sixty years, *colored* was embraced by black people as a symbol of pride and freedom, as evidenced by its use in the name of the NAACP (the National Association for the Advancement of *Colored* People), founded in 1909 to assist blacks in their struggle for social equality. By the 1930s, however, the name *colored* began losing ground to the re-emergent, newly capitalized *Negro*. And by mid-century, *colored* was completely outmoded. "During the civil rights movement of the 1950s and 1960s, it was *Negro* that speakers and writers most often chose, whether they were expressing racial pride or demanding social justice."[52] It was also *Negro* that quickly became unsuitable for the younger, more militant followers of the Black Power movement of the late 1960s and early 1970s. They found that the labels *black* and *Afro-American* were much better descriptors of a people who were proud of their black culture and sought to celebrate their African heritage. They wore Afro hairstyles, draped themselves in dashikis (West African–style shirts), adorned their necks with ornaments and medallions, and echoed the words of James Brown's 1968 hit single "Say It Loud – I'm Black and I'm Proud." But in the following decades, as *black* maintained its popularity, *Afro-American* gave way to a term that was promoted by Jesse Jackson and other black leaders in the late 1980s: African American. All in all, *colored, Negro, black, Afro-American,* and *African American* have each had their own historical moment of legitimacy in the black community.

*Nigger* has never had such a moment. Its divisive and destructive trek began well before the end of American slavery. As early as the 1830s, *nigger* had already become such a familiar and influential insult that the prominent black abolitionist, minister, and lecturer Hosea Easton (1837) described it as "an opprobrious term, employed to impose contempt upon [blacks] as an inferior race … It flows from the fountain of purpose to injure."[53] But what does *nigger* actually mean? And how did it attain its derogatory connotation?

Most lexicographers trace the word to *niger,* the Latin word meaning "black in color." Some also contend that *nigger* did not originate as a racial slur but began as a neutral term[54] that eventually became what Christopher Darden (the prosecuting attorney in the O. J. Simpson murder trial of 1995) describes as the "filthiest, dirtiest, nastiest word in the English language."[55] Jabari Asim (2007) explains that this contention (that *nigger* began as a neutral term) is based mainly on "[the neutral use] of 'nigers' in the 'learned discourse' of the seventeenth-century anti-slavery activist Samuel Sewall, [suggesting] that the word acquired a derogatory character over time, picking up various spellings along the way."[56] As such, the insatiable fire that continues to rage under the surface of the label *nigger* (even in 2008) was undoubtedly sparked and fed by the overwhelming negative usage of the label between the 1600s and the 1800s. European slave traders of the early 1600s consistently referred to their African captives as *niggers*. Jamestown colonist John Rolfe even wrote in his diary in 1619 of the first shipment of *negars* to the new territory.[57]

From these meager beginnings and over the next two hundred years, the already offensive label slowly found its way into popular songs, poems, jokes, nursery rhymes, literature, and especially into everyday language.[58] Common expressions of the period included *nigger baby*, referring to "a large artillery projectile"; *nigger bean*, referring to "a dark-colored bean"; *niggerish*, meaning "shiftless or no-account"; *nigger-knocker*, referring to "a club used as a weapon against blacks"; *nigger news*, meaning "gossip"; *nigger out*, meaning "to back out of an agreement"; and *nigger-shooter*, referring to "a slingshot."[59] These few expressions alone offer great insight into the vile history, nature, and meaning of the word *nigger*. And yet, young black males use this term (in the form of *nigga*) as if it were as neutral as the word *brother*.

Again, what lucid people would take a weapon from a defeated enemy and destroy themselves with it? Our black boys would have us believe that they have seized ownership of evil (*nigger*) and transformed it into good (*nigga*). They would certainly argue that *nigga* is a beautiful thing when used between "brothers." U.S. Supreme Court Justice Oliver Wendell Holmes (1918) once remarked that a word "is the skin of a living thought [that] may vary greatly in color and content according to the circumstances and the time in which it is used."[60] Although Justice Holmes makes a very astute observation, no one of credibility can logically conclude that there has been a significant transformative change in the meaning of the word *nigger* (in the form of *nigga*) among black males. It seems that the black male peer group has succeeded only in repackaging an old abomination, making it an attractive, acceptable, and indispensable part of black culture. In other words, by referring to each other as *nigga*, our black boys are now nicely saying about each other what white racists have viciously said about them.

Anyone who doubts the similarity of meanings between *nigger* and *nigga* need only determine how black males themselves define *nigga*, an assessment easily made by simply perusing the lyrics of their designated spokespersons, gangsta rappers. In "3 Peat" (2008), Lil Wayne claims that if he were so provoked, he could easily "run up in [a] niggas house and shoot his grandmother up."[61] T.I. reveals in "Ready for Whatever" (2008) that he spends $500,000 a year on security to stave off those "niggas out there plottin' to rob and kill [him]."[62] Throughout the song "Money Make Me Come" (2008), Rick Ross refers to black women as *bitches* and *hoe niggas*.[63] In "Everything" (2008), Young Jeezy takes great pride in the fact that he is a "real street nigga" who was born "hard" and will die "hard."[64] Plies explains in "Worth Goin FED Fo" (2008) that if you "take the streets from a nigga then a nigga [will] starve."[65] And in "My Life" (2008), The Game brags, "[he] spit crack and niggas … drive it outta town."[66] These excerpts, taken from among the top-ten selling rap albums of 2008,[67] give us a clear understanding of how the black male peer group defines niggas: stupid, lazy, dangerous, hypersexual dregs of society whose value is measured more by the degree to which they benefit "the crew" than by their intrinsic humanity. Does this definition not coalesce well with the traditional meaning of *nigger*? By using the word *nigga*, therefore, our black boys are deliberately embracing a word (*nigger*) that is still pregnant with the remnants of a long history of racism, servitude, and subjugation.

Young black males are so attached to this disparaging label that any alternative pales in comparison. In no uncertain terms, if you are not a *nigga*, with all that it entails, then in the eyes of the black male peer group you are either a sellout or an Uncle Tom. The choice is simple: *be down with the brothers* and receive the badge of *nigga*, or be disrespected and ostracized by the "brothers" as a sellout. This entrenched cultural ultimatum has made the word *nigga* a natural part of the black dialect. And our black boys use this epithet among themselves and in the presence of nonblacks with such novel ease and frequency that they not only diminish their own self-concept, but they diminish their ability to stigmatize the word (whether in the form of *nigga* or *nigger*) when used by whites. As Randall Kennedy states in *Nigger* (2003), "The more aware judges and other officials become of the [perceived] ambiguity surrounding 'nigger', the less likely they will be to automatically condemn the actions taken by whites who voice the N-word."[68]

But even more to the point, how can a group of people embrace a word so fully and completely and then forbid its usage by others? Does a father who smokes two packs of cigarettes every day have any moral standing to tell his child not to smoke? Was it hypocritical for blacks to brazenly criticize Jennifer Lopez for her use of *nigga* in her 2002 song "I'm Real"?[69] Is it fair for Eminem, perhaps the most "accepted" white rapper in rap history, to feel so duty bound never to use any form of *nigger* in his songs or otherwise?[70] Was it a travesty of justice in 1999 for Anthony Williams, the newly elected mayor of Washington DC, to ask for the resignation of his ombudsman, David Howard (a white man), for his innocent use of the word *niggardly* (a word that is historically unrelated to *nigger*) when he referred to a need to be frugal with certain city funds?[71]

For young black males, these scenarios are exactly as they should be, because it is they, and they alone, who now claim ownership of what was once the *white man's serpent* (*nigger*). But what have they done with it? They have sweetened its poison, refined its image, and accepted its evil as a "gift" to their peer group.

## Summary

In short, our black boys make up the rank and file of a peer group that is bent on total self-destruction—a peer group that lays all of its troubles at the feet of racism (the weakest excuse for failure in twenty-first-century America),[72] fatherlessness, and educational malpractice, taking no responsibility for itself. Certainly, black males have suffered at the hands of the family and the school system. In fact, much of their self-destructive mentality is a direct result of that mistreatment. But human beings are not automatons that can be programmed for *inevitable* success or *inevitable* failure. Choice, even in the worst of circumstances, is always a factor. If this were not the case, then how could someone who was born in the segregated South of the 1940s to a poor, unwed teenage mother and an absent, noninvolved father become anything other than a scourge on society? And yet, these were Jesse Jackson's beginnings. As a child, he endured painful rejection at every turn: (1) from society at large in the form of racism and discrimination; (2) from his biological father, a thirty-two-year-old next-door neighbor who had his own family and no time for Jesse; and (3) from the black community itself, which, at that time, did not look too favorably upon children of unwed mothers.[73] So, before Jackson became part of Dr. Martin Luther King, Jr.'s inner circle in 1966, before he became the national director of Operation Breadbasket (an economic improvement organization for blacks) in 1967, before he started Operation PUSH (People United to Save Humanity) in 1971, and before he founded the National Rainbow Coalition and ran for president of the United States in 1984 and 1988, he had to make a childhood choice to place his life on a positive path in the face of what may have seemed to be insurmountable odds.

Our black boys today have no excuses. They *choose* to follow the dictates of a peer group that leads its members directly to failure, prison, and death. There is no other way to explain why a whole nation of young "brothers" accept the label *nigger* (in the form of *nigga*) with open arms, why they act out negative racial stereotypes to demonstrate their manhood, or why they have such a deep admiration for career criminals and prison life.

# 4
# The Influence of the Mass Media

*It is impossible to live in peace with*
*those whom we believe to be damned.*

—Jean-Jacques Rousseau

In contrast to the family, the school system, and the peer group, the assertion that the mass media is an influential and essential agency of socialization has been, and continues to be, viewed by many as no more than supposition. And yet sociologists have made it abundantly clear that it is often through the mass media that children are first introduced to many aspects of culture (aspects perhaps not conferred by the family) and many "ways of society."[1] *A Modern Dictionary of Sociology* (1969) defines *mass media* (a term coined in the 1920s) as "any means or instrument of communication reaching large numbers of people, such as books, periodicals, radio, television, motion pictures,"[2] and, in recent years, the Internet. Through this powerful collection of media, children are "taught," however misleadingly, (1) about the duties of people in particular roles, (2) about the functions of major institutions in society, (3) about the appropriate behavior required in given social situations, and (4) about the relationships that exist between status positions.[3] It is also through the mass media that children are inundated with a steady stream of positive and negative messages about such topics as racial differences, gender roles, religious tolerance, cultural diversity, sexual norms, sexual orientation, and family structure. Hence, the real strength of this communications-based agency of socialization lies in its ability to effectively shape public attitudes and opinions.[4]

Unfortunately, with all of its power and influence, the predominantly white-controlled American mass media has rarely been kind to black males. Even before our black boys began their own campaign of self-destruction (through their peer group), an image of them and their forefathers as being genetically inferior, criminal-prone, sex-crazed, violent degenerates had already been carefully crafted and utilized,[5] not only as a means of maintaining control over the very lucrative slave-driven commercial farming industry of the antebellum South, but also as a method of preserving white social and political power during much of the nineteenth (after Reconstruction) and twentieth centuries. Today, *the fine art of black-male bashing* still continues via a so-called "new and improved" mass media (incorporating white liberals and black-owned media outlets)—one that is motivated less by the old racism, and more by the old racial stereotypes that are now used to build careers, fill business coffers, and promote political interests.

## Maintaining Control of a Lucrative Industry

Throughout American history, greed played a profoundly important role in the objectification and defamation of people of African descent. For example, the African slave trade and the products created by African slave labor between the 1660s and the 1860s provided the basis for America's wealth as a nation, underwrote the country's industrial revolution, and enabled it to project its power into the rest of the world.[6] And a large part of the rationale for this unsolicited exploitation was the English perception that Africans were a subhuman species made for servitude. Hence, if greed has been the fuel for media-based black-male bashing, racism, at least initially, was the vehicle. In fact, more than a half-century before the first successful English colony was established (Jamestown in 1607), English voyagers on trading missions (unrelated to slavery) found themselves face-to-face with "peculiar," dark-skinned West African natives. It was during these introductory contacts that ethnocentrism, and eventually racism, began to congeal in the English mind, well before British colonial slavery was even an issue.[7]

In *The White Man's Burden* (1974), Winthrop D. Jordan highlights several African characteristics that Englishmen had difficulty reconciling with their Northwestern European experiences and modes of thinking, leading directly to their negative perceptions of people of African descent. The first and most arresting characteristic of the newly discovered African was his "blackness," which, for the English, was a badge of evil and impurity, a symbol of depravity and debauchery, and a sign of danger and dysfunction.[8] The "fact," therefore, that these dark-colored people were un-Christian, "heathen, libidinous savages" who displayed "bestial" and even "ape-like" behavior was simply par for the course.[9] So, for one hundred years—after the first contacts with West Africans were made in the 1550s and before British colonial slavery had officially begun in the 1660s—this racist image of black people slowly seeped into the social fabric of English society (including their established colonies), giving the American proslavery mass media of much of the subsequent slave period (c. 1662–1865) plenty of fodder to conduct its mission of absolving slavery supporters and reinforcing control over what became a very lucrative industry.

Although a *legitimate* mass media was effectively nonexistent in America before the Revolutionary period (1763–1783) due to high illiteracy rates, privation, and a lack of widespread demand for newspapers (or other forms of media),[10] the groundwork for public black-male bashing had already been laid as *race* became *the* single determinant of one's fate. In other words, between 1660 and 1700, *white* (a new term of self-identification) had become synonymous with *freedom*, and *black* had become synonymous with *enslavement*. Hence, the foundation of chattel *racial* slavery and its ensuing defenses were established.[11] John Saffin, who was a prominent Massachusetts lawyer and statesman, and a slave owner and trader himself, authored one of the earliest proslavery documents on record.[12] In *A Brief, Candid Answer to a Late Printed Sheet, Entitled, The Selling of Joseph* (1701), a calculated response to one of his antislavery contemporaries, Saffin, in no uncertain terms asked his readers to consider several pointed questions: (1) How can slavery be wrong if Abraham, the first patriarch of the Jews, Christians, and Muslims, owned slaves? (2) How can slavery be wrong if it offers heathen Africans the opportunity to become civilized Christians? (3) And how can slavery be wrong if the enslaved, themselves, are innately defective and inferior?[13] So, for John Saffin and many other pre-Revolution defenders of slavery (e.g., Cotton Mather, Stephen Hales, George Whitefield, and Thomas Bacon), forced African labor was not only necessary for growing colonial economies, but it was highly beneficial to Africans who were no more than "poor ignorant creatures, who [had] little or no care taken of their principles; little or no notion of an all-seeing God, or a future judgment; nothing but sense and appetite to guide them; nothing but the present object to allure or terrify them."[14] Ironically, as most white colonists began to fathom their own independence and freedom from the strong hand of British rule, it was this *positive good* philosophy of slavery (based on the degradation of black people) that became the rallying cry of many proslavery propagandists who found solace and power in a burgeoning mass media. Through sermons, broadsides, pamphlets, poetry, plays, almanacs, popular songs, and, especially, newspapers, the racial prejudices of what was soon to be an autonomous nation were laid bare.[15]

Between 1763 and 1783, as "Americans" sought and won the right to govern themselves, several concomitant factors provided for the makings of a vast, influential mass media and an unprecedented era (up until that time) of black-male bashing: (1) colonies grew substantially in size as economic opportunity, generous land policies, and religious freedom attracted many European immigrants during the latter third of the eighteenth century;[16] (2) the proportion of blacks in the colonies surged from 4 percent in 1700 to nearly 40 percent by 1770 due to larger white populations, increased landownership, and a sustained demand for field labor;[17] (3) the inconsistency of white Americans demanding freedom for themselves (from British oppression) while denying freedom to other human beings spurred the development of antislavery sentiment and, hence, the need for slaveholders to publicly justify their "peculiar institution";[18] and (4) American newspapers were establishing themselves as indispensable organs of home-grown political and social opinions as literacy rates improved dramatically (especially among women) and as higher populations created higher circulations.[19] After 1763, proslavery propaganda flooded the print media (such as it was) as slave owners and their apologists scrambled to assuage rising opposition. In that vein, the vast majority of colonial newspapers focused heavily on reporting alleged black conspiracies, incidents of black lawbreaking, and plantation owners' accounts of "corrupted" runaway slaves at large, characterizing blacks as having a penchant for disobedience, violence, and criminality.[20] The fact is, "Black virtue was seldom acknowledged in the public prints, even in the limited spheres where it was allowed to exist."[21]

It stands to reason, therefore, that most of the mass media was, at the very least, strongly influenced by proslavery factions. News weeklies (daily newspapers did not exist until 1783)[22] like the *Boston Gazette*, the *Boston Evening-Post*, the *Virginia Gazette*, and the *South-Carolina Gazette* printed a steady stream of stories, sermons, and advertisements illustrating the lawless indiscretions of slaves, which were meant not only as warnings to slaveholders to keep a tighter reign on their "servants," but primarily as messages to the general public that no institution was better suited for the untrustworthy, violence-prone African than slavery.[23] So, for defenders of slavery during the Revolutionary period, media-based black-male bashing had become a means to a *positive good* end.

Even in the midst of political, social, and ideological transformation (1776–1789) that included the achievement of America's national sovereignty (marked by the signing of the Treaty of Paris on September 3, 1783), the mindset of proslavery propagandists remained relatively unchanged. If anything, this acrimonious bunch became more emboldened during the last decade of the eighteenth century as *sectionalism* bore upon the fledgling union of ex-British colonies.[24] Although sectional division in the 1790s lacked the clarity it was to take on in the 1850s and 1860s, the reasons for sectional discord and regional conflict were proven to be absolutely timeless. Because the American Revolution bolstered antislavery sentiment and brought freedom to vast numbers of slaves as a war expedient, many Americans became convinced that slavery was not only a dying institution, but that it was sorely out of place in a new nation being built on the principles of freedom.[25]

Of course, the predominance of this ideology was based primarily on three regional factors: (1) the proportion of blacks in the particular region, (2) the profitability of slavery in the region, and (3) the degree of abolitionist meddling in the region.[26] In the North (those states north of Maryland and Delaware), for example, the concentration of blacks remained relatively low because there was little profit in owning slaves in a climate that was not conducive to high crop yields—a fact assuring that every Northern state would eventually (by 1804) abolish slavery outright or enact plans for gradual emancipation.[27] In the Upper

South (those states south of Pennsylvania and north of South Carolina), even with its fair climate and high concentration of blacks, crop production was stable but not highly profitable; however, significant economic reward was found in selling superfluous slaves to the Lower South. It was the Lower South (those states south of North Carolina) that had the most agreeable climate, the highest proportion of blacks, and that profited most from slavery—particularly after the introduction of Eli Whitney's cotton gin in 1793.[28] As such, to maintain its lucrative industry and indeed its very way of life, the South (especially the Lower South) defended its "peculiar institution" well into the nineteenth century *by any means necessary*—from public black-male bashing to all-out civil war.

At the onset of the new century, therefore, economic reinvigoration, sectional discord, abolitionist meddling, and a genuine fear of slave revolts gave further motivation to an already unyielding proslavery mass media—one given apparent legitimacy by the dominant, influential voices of well-respected clergymen.[29] Edmund Botsford, a successful itinerant Baptist minister from South Carolina, was a good example. In his proslavery tract *Sambo and Toney* (1808), Botsford highlighted, in fictive form, the duties of religious white masters to Christianize and care for their slaves and, reciprocally, of slaves to accept their "God-given" station in life and be good and faithful servants to their masters.[30] In short order, Botsford's message was widely echoed by many other Southern Christian proselytizers, like the evangelical Episcopal priest William Meade (1813), who insisted that the master–slave relationship *could* reflect the principles of Christianity wherein great importance would be placed on providing religious instruction to "our ignorant fellow-creatures."[31]

This wholesale defense of slavery using Biblical principles was certainly nothing new to American society, but it did become a more popular and acceptable practice after the Great Revival of 1801 (the religious awakening of the South) and even more so after the coincident inception of William Lloyd Garrison's pro-abolitionist *Liberator* and the insurrection of Nat Turner in 1831.[32] Racist, religious, proslavery ideologies under the guise of Christian benevolence now had a firm foothold in the slavery-entrenched South. And Thornton Stringfellow, a prominent, well-known Virginia Baptist minister, epitomized and validated this Southern sense of self-righteousness via his highly acclaimed, widely distributed proslavery publication *A Brief Examination of the Scripture Testimony on the Institution of Slavery* (1841). In essence, Stringfellow gave his proslavery contemporaries an authoritative catalog of scriptural references that would be used throughout the Civil War to defend the *positive good* institution of slavery and further degrade the African who was, after all, "created for servitude."[33] Hence, chattel *racial* slavery and its ardent apologists (i.e., many novelists, biologists, economists, statesmen, and especially ministers of the gospel), like Botsford, Meade, and Stringfellow, created an image of black people that is still a part of the American mindset in 2008. Proslavery-based propaganda, by its own definition, died at the close of the Civil War (1865), but the proslavery themes of racial subjugation and debasement survived the "peculiar institution" by more than one hundred years.

## Preserving White Social and Political Power

Although white Southerners lost the Civil War and had to endure what they considered a "nigger-serving" Radical Reconstruction (1867–1877), their determination to protect their social, political, and economic power—and the "integrity" of their white women—from "the ignorant, incompetent, predatory Negro" gave them a postwar motivation to continue their prewar practice of media-based black-male bashing. This, of course, came as part of a larger tapestry of approaches that was used to bombard the four million newly freed "uppity Negroes" (Southern blacks made up 91 percent of the total black population of the United States in 1870)[34] in an effort to keep them in their inferior, subservient place. The most extreme and effective approach was outright violence. By 1870, such vigilante political terrorist groups as the Ku Klux Klan, the Knights of the White Camelia, and the White Brotherhood existed in nearly every Southern state, and they participated regularly in the beating and lynching of blacks who they felt "stepped out of line."[35]

In a broader sense, major violent incidents sponsored by these types of vigilante hate groups, like the Colfax Massacre (1873) and Coushatta murders (1874) of blacks and white Republicans in Louisiana, provided the impetus for the gradual dismantling of Reconstruction as they laid the groundwork for several Supreme Court decisions that in effect re-empowered local and state authorities in Southern states to handle their own affairs without federal intervention. These developments, along with the so-called Mississippi Plan of 1875 (copied and utilized successfully throughout the South), which used various forms of intimidation to usurp the vote and political power from *scalawags* (white Southerners who supported the federal government) and blacks, led directly to the Compromise of 1877 and the final death knell for Radical Reconstruction.[36]

So, during the last twenty-three years of the nineteenth century, as white Southerners regained racial control, and as black Southerners were pushed back almost to the brink of slavery, the primary major mass entertainment medium in America (North and South) was the minstrel stage, which provided in ornate theaters and in the tents of traveling shows what populist audiences demanded: blacks depicted as naïve, mischievous, "massuh lovin'" buffoons who sang and danced the days away.[37]

The importance of minstrelsy as a symbol of the time cannot be overstated. Unlike many newspapers, magazines, scientific journals, political tracts, and religious publications of the period, the minstrel show was not necessarily created as a tool of propaganda, but primarily as a product of public expectations.[38] In other words, the vast majority of white Americans, from the northernmost Federalist Republican to the southernmost Confederate Democrat, delighted in the foolhardy, stereotypical antics of white and black performers donned in blackface because they shared a perception of the Negro that emerged from an America diseased with bigotry and racism. In fact, according to the *The Encyclopedia of New York City* (1995), homegrown (American born and bred) blackface acts were common features in circuses and traveling shows from the 1790s onward.[39] But it was minstrel pioneers like Thomas "Daddy" Rice (1828), the Christy Minstrels (1843), the Virginia Minstrels (1843), Brooker and Clayton's Georgia Minstrels (1865), Callender's Original Georgia Minstrels (1872), Kersands' Colored Minstrels (1885), and W. S. Cleveland's Colored Minstrels (1890) that made the lampooning of Negroes in blackface America's entertainment staple during a time when Jim Crow laws (passed by eight Southern states by 1891)[40] took center stage and *separate but equal* (1896) officially replaced *proslavery* as the new calling card for the justification of *nationwide* race-based maltreatment and media-based black-male bashing.

Whites were determined to maintain their social, political, and economic superiority at all costs. As the nineteenth century came to a close, racism remained embedded in major U.S. institutions; the majority of the media, through their commentary and reportage, continued to promote the idea legitimized by our own Founding Fathers (e.g., George Washington, John Adams, Thomas Jefferson, and James Madison)[41] that blacks were indeed different from whites as defined by their work ethic, intelligence, patriotism, and civility;[42] and the medium of minstrelsy, as it was further popularized by Al Jolson (until the late 1920s), continued to reflect the stereotypical preferences of a demanding white public.[43] The tone of the new century was set. The continuance of the existing system of racial stratification through the oppression and disparagement of black people was an absolute priority if white social, political, and economic power was to be preserved.

By 1900, as the common man enjoyed the residual benefits of American industrialization (cresting between 1860 and 1890)[44] and the freedoms and comforts associated with increased technology, it was all too obvious that the common man was not black. In the Northern states, "Blacks, with few exceptions, were proscribed from employment in all but menial laboring and personal-service positions."[45] In the South, whites filled the factories, mills, and mines, while Negroes remained captive to the trinity of cotton, tenancy, and poverty.[46] The vast majority of blacks also remained disenfranchised and barred from all manner of public accommodations, and nearly 50 percent of them were still illiterate, compared to only 6 percent of whites.[47]

Of course, according to so-called reputable early twentieth-century academics, these depressing conditions, along with the lingering horrors of unjustified lynchings (claiming the lives of more than two thousand blacks between 1881 and 1901),[48] were exactly what the "lowly Negro" deserved. In *"The Negro a Beast" or "In the Image of God"* (1900), Charles Carroll, a renowned scholar and scientist, argued that the white man was the last act of creation (Adam and Eve were white), making the Negro a pre-Adam subspecies of the animal kingdom—akin to the ape.[49] Another prominent thinker of the period, William P. Calhoun, suggested in *The Caucasian and the Negro in the United States* (1902) that unless the naturally inept Negro was completely separated from direct competition with the more superior white man, the Negro would most certainly be doomed to inevitable extermination through his own failures.[50] William B. Smith, a professor of mathematics at Tulane University in New Orleans, seconded Calhoun's suggestion in his book *The Color Line: A Brief in Behalf of the Unborn* (1905).[51] And to add fuel to the fire, Robert W. Shufeldt, a retired military doctor and a member of the National Geographic Society, proclaimed in *The Negro: A Menace to American Civilization* (1907) that blacks are "purely animal" with no morals and no concern for posterity or progressive civilization. They are so bestial, in fact, according to Shufeldt, that "all [of their] passions, emotions, and ambitions are almost wholly subservient to [their] sensual instinct."[52] Much like the well-respected proslavery clergymen of the early 1800s, Carroll, Calhoun, Smith, Shufeldt, and many of their "distinguished" contemporaries legitimated an already accepted image of the Negro, strengthening the resolve of an unconscionable, unrestrained mass media between 1900 and 1930.

A two-hundred-year tradition of unadulterated black-male bashing continued unabated. Newspapers like the *New York Times*, the *Chicago Tribune*, the *Boston Evening Transcript*, the *San Francisco Examiner*, and *Harper's Weekly* "heisted the lingo from the academics and had great fun ridiculing, lampooning, butchering, and assailing black men in articles and cartoons."[53] The black male image did not fare much better in popular magazines. The *Century Magazine*, the *Atlantic Monthly*, the *North American Review*, and *Popular Science Monthly*, for example, embraced many of the accepted racial stereotypes through national advertising (an essential source of revenue for magazines beginning around 1900) and reporting.[54]

The pervasive conception of the morally corrupt, shiftless, imbecilic, brutish Negro, perpetuated by a host of magazines, newspapers, and other forms of print media, was also well represented in landmark films of the early twentieth century. Perhaps the most controversial and racially incendiary motion picture ever made was the feature-length, technical epic *The Birth of a Nation* (1915), the first blockbuster (10 percent of the U.S. population attended its original release) in silent film history. It portrayed the black man as a naturally inferior, criminal-prone, sex-crazed beast who had to be tamed by the "virtuous" Ku Klux

Klan.[55] Even the comparatively racially mild-mannered first *talkie* (a film with sound), *The Jazz Singer*, debuting as a box office hit in 1927, prominently displayed the patently racist symbol of the minstrel mask (*blackface*) as donned by the preeminent blackface entertainer, and star of the film, Al Jolson. Ironically, it was the release of *The Jazz Singer* (1927) that marked the time period in which motion pictures began to supplant the live stage show in popularity.[56] As such, by the time *Gone With the Wind* graced the theaters in 1939, showcasing the stereotypical "faithful mammy" and the "happy, lazy slave," the American public was used to Hollywood depicting blacks as slaves, peons, and underlings delighted with their servile roles.[57] During this pre-television (before television became a major mass medium) motion picture era, between 1930 and 1945, while white attitudes toward blacks had not changed, media-based black-male bashing did eventually take on a more modified, politically correct tone in order to conform to the "new" realities of *the multidimensional Negro*. "The movie industry's response to [these 'new' social realities] was simply to shift to new stereotypes that were still consistent with prejudicial notions."[58] By the end of World War II (1945), the black man was still considered "the beast" of society.

Wartime scientists and scholars may have succeeded in discrediting the old racialist theories of black inferiority, but the myth of black hypersexuality continued to linger; negative images of Negroes in corporate advertising continued to flourish; and news headlines and text were continuously filled with racial epithets directed toward blacks, especially when reporting incidents of racial conflict.[59] Even in the midst of unprecedented social improvements between 1949 and 1972, blacks still encountered systematic and overt discrimination in employment, education, and housing. They endured sanctions, punishment, and social exclusion for breaking anti-miscegenation laws that were passed and enforced by thirty of forty-eight states as of 1945. And they were subjected to a racially hostile, albeit much more tame, mass media that, in effect, maintained and fueled the *us versus them* public mentality.[60] As far as the majority was concerned, white power and privilege were to be preserved despite the incremental advances made by Negroes during this historic period.

Nonetheless, those who sought to keep blacks impotent and oppressed indefinitely were soon proven to be delusional. By 1973, there were more black mayors and U.S. congressmen serving American cities and districts than at any time since the turn of the century. The number of blacks in poverty fell substantially, while overall black family income rose to its highest level ever.[61] Several civil rights acts, a voting rights act, and a fair housing act were passed and signed into law. Mandated de jure segregation in public facilities—"Jim Crowism"—was a thing of the past. And in 1967, the U.S. Supreme Court declared antimiscegenation laws unconstitutional.[62]

But in what ways had the use of the mass media changed in light of the preceding social revolution (c. 1949–1972)? Although the mass media has always had an influence on public opinion, public opinion has, likewise, had an influence on how the mass media has been utilized, and white attitudes toward blacks had changed significantly by the mid-1970s. Whites no longer viewed blacks as being necessarily innately inferior or as being completely socially unacceptable.[63] Thus, through the media, entrepreneurs, politicians, journalists, and powerbrokers (black and white) began to hang their economic, political, and social hats less on the blistering racist montages of the past, and more on the stereotypical constant—the stupid, lazy, dangerous, hypersexual black man.

## Exploiting the Remnants of Racism

The time-tested polarizing remnants of three hundred years of racism became tools of expedience for those opportunists and profiteers who understood how to use the seemingly omnipotent, omnipresent American media to exploit those tools. They had at their disposal in the 1970s, and beyond, a system of mass communication unlike that of any other time in U.S. history. Newspapers, magazines, radio, television, and motion pictures formed the cornerstone of that system. Due to the advent of radio and television, the newspaper industry was certainly not what it once was, but as of 1975, there were still 1,756 daily newspapers in operation, and 72 percent of adults still read newspapers on a daily basis.[64] In the late 1950s and early 1960s, magazines also suffered setbacks because of the popularity of television programming and commercial television advertising. However, through advances in production and printing technology (improving profitability) and a strong focus on niche publishing (serving the specific informational needs of particular segments of the population), the magazine industry, as a whole, rallied and prospered well into the 1990s.[65] Analogously, network radio maintained its viability and its long-standing relationship with the American public (since 1927) in spite of losing many of its established stars to network television.

In fact, the FCC reported that as of March 31, 1979, there were 8,651 radio stations on the air, 4,549 AM and 4,102 FM, and that 98 percent of all U.S. households contained at least one radio set. Not surprisingly, the television-to-household figures were equally impressive.[66] Meanwhile, alongside radio and television, the motion picture had not only maintained its nationwide popularity since *The Jazz Singer* was released in 1927, but the American film industry dominated the *world* market throughout the twentieth century.[67]

Newspapers, magazines, radio, television, and motion pictures, each unique and influential in their own right, together formed a media monolith that reflected political, economic, and social trends informed by strong public opinions and general racial attitudes. So, what was the general racial attitude of the majority of Americans—white Americans—beginning in the mid-1970s? And how did that general attitude affect how the mass media was used from that point forward?

According to a study conducted by D. Garth Taylor et al. (1978), there was a remarkable liberal leap forward in racial tolerance in the North and the South between 1970 and 1972, followed by steady positive change between 1972 and 1976. These findings of Taylor and his colleagues were based on a nationwide sample of about 1,350 whites that were asked questions concerning school integration, neighborhood composition, personal racial interactions, antimiscegenation laws, and *forced* desegregation.[68] In a review of related literature, the Division of Behavioral and Social Sciences and Education (DBASSE) of the National Research Council (NRC) also concluded in *A Common Destiny* (1989) that the 1970s brought sharp upturns in positive attitudes among whites on issues of social and civil liberties, whether such attitudinal shifts were the result of dramatic changes in the historical context (e.g., an increase in social awareness through a general rise in social protest) or the natural process of generation replacement.[69] More specifically, the DBASSE found that "the once widespread acceptance of segregation and discrimination as the guiding principles of black–white relations [had] given way to acceptance of the principles of desegregation and equal treatment."[70]

But as promising and progressive as this new racial tone was, it did come with specific stipulations having to do with *racial proxemics* (changes in white racial attitudes based on the level of racial exposure). To test the theory of racial proxemics, a Gallup poll was conducted in 1958 and again in 1978 asking white respondents a series of questions that took into account hypothetical levels of black–white contact in public schools and in residential areas. The Gallup data suggested that although white opinions of blacks improved significantly over the twenty-year period, "principles of equality [were] endorsed less when social contact [was] close, of long duration, or frequent and when it involved significant numbers of blacks."[71] In other words, in 1978—and even in 2008—many of the same whites who *earnestly* believed that racial discrimination had no place in American society would abandon a school system or leave a neighborhood if they felt that they or their children were overexposed to blacks.[72] The only way to explain this seeming disconnect between white social thought and white social behavior is to admit that negative black stereotypes still lingered in the American mindset, notwithstanding the historic improvements in racial tolerance.

*Black* remained synonymous with *stupid, lazy, dangerous,* and *hypersexual.*

Ironically, these stereotypical constants, which were once used to maintain control of a lucrative, slave-driven industry and to help render millions of Negroes socially and politically powerless for countless decades after slavery, were now used as part of an effective formula for building careers, generating wealth, and advancing politically. One of the best examples of this new mode of operation was the creation and perpetuation of the appropriately labeled *blaxploitation* film genre of the early 1970s. Cheaply made, poorly acted, white-funded and controlled blaxploitation niche films could not be categorized as racist because the black main character almost always prevailed over the oppressive white system.[73] But they were replete with the standard black male stereotypes. Movies like *Sweet Sweetback's Baadasssss Song* (1971), *Super Fly* (1972), *Coffy* (1973), *The Black Godfather* (1974), *Willie Dynamite* (1974), and *Dolemite* (1975) portrayed black men as law-flouting, smooth-talking, flashy-dressing pimps, drug dealers, and mobsters who used violence and intimidation to maintain their power and reputation. Out of the fifteen or so films released each year between 1971 and 1974 by white-owned distribution companies, an estimated 25 percent of them were of the blaxploitation genre, as white filmmakers were well aware of the need in the black community for big-screen heroes who thumbed their noses at the system and won.[74] As such, during the first half of the 1970s, black-oriented films exuding sex, violence, and "super-cool" individualism were considered cash cows within the motion picture industry. By 1975, however, "when Hollywood no longer needed its cheap black product line for its economic survival,"[75] the short-lived blaxploitation film era came to an end, despite the continued exploitation of the black male image by white and black filmmakers in motion pictures like *Penitentiary* (1979), *The Big Score* (1983), *I'm Gonna Git You Sucka* (1988), *Boyz N the Hood* (1991), *Juice* (1992), *Menace II Society* (1993), *Original Gangsters* (1996), and *Full Clip* (2004). As was the case within other major mass mediums, in the film industry, the use of black stereotypes assured that pockets remained filled and that careers remained buoyant.

Newspapers and magazines were no exception. Their pages were almost always littered with stories and reports that catered to white public expectations of black people. One primary piece of misinformation, for example, that has been consistently buttressed by the press was that the majority of blacks were desperately poor (i.e., poverty stricken) and resided in dilapidated urban ghettos—furtively promoting the idea that black people were generally stupid and lazy. This widespread misconception has been especially disturbing in light of the actual facts. Surely, the percentage of blacks in poverty almost always surpassed that of any other racial or ethnic group. But since 1968, the black poverty rate has never exceeded 36 percent, and today it hovers closer to 24 percent—a far cry from a majority.[76]

A similar argument can be made about the presumption that most blacks live in ghetto neighborhoods. While it is true that for the last forty years blacks have consistently represented the largest segment of those who live in high-poverty areas (from 59 percent in 1970 to less than 39 percent today), it is also true that these same blacks have consistently represented less than 15 percent of the total black population.[77] Again, there is no evidence of a majority. And yet, newspapers and magazines continued to subscribe to the clearly unfounded but highly popular stereotype of the poverty-stricken, ghetto-dwelling black man. According to Martin Gilens (1999), news coverage of the poor between the 1950s and early 1960s was meager and predominantly white-centered. But after the tumultuous years of the mid-1960s and the impetus of the Johnson administration's War on Poverty (begun in 1964), poverty, itself, took on a black face.[78] In an analysis of forty-two years (1950–1992) of newsmagazine pictures of the poor, Gilens found that more than 50 percent (up to 84 percent) of pictures presented with stories pertaining to *urban problems*, *poor people and poverty*, *unemployment*, *welfare*, and *homelessness* prominently displayed the faces of black people.[79] So, without a doubt, the decade of the 1970s (as well as the late 1960s) gave media-based black-male bashing a new place and purpose in American society. And no group of people understood this better than self-serving, power-hungry politicians.

As Clarence Page stated in his book *Showing My Color* (1996), "the demonization of blacks through racially coded appeals to white fears became a standard feature" of the conservative counterculture that emerged in the late 1960s.[80] Essentially, race-baiting, fueled by the "intolerable antics" of Negro race rioters, civil rights agitators, and antiwar demonstrators, became the new weapon of war in the arsenal of many political campaigns. George Wallace, a quintessential racist and former governor of Alabama, was one of the first to demonstrate its effective usage in his bid for the presidency in 1968. Running as a third-party candidate, Wallace derided federal intervention, mandated integration, and forced busing. And for all of his race-baiting efforts, he garnered nearly ten million votes (14 percent of the popular vote) and won five Southern states—"the best showing by a third-party candidate since La Follette in 1924."[81]

George Wallace may not have won the presidency, but he certainly showed others how to win. In fact, Richard Nixon won the 1968 contest by appealing to a message of *law and order* in the midst of what he considered escalating violence of "the poor, the ignorant, and the irresponsible." Ronald Reagan beat Jimmy Carter handily in 1980 by attacking affirmative action and "welfare queens."[82] George Bush would win in 1988 by successfully connecting his opponent, Governor Michael Dukakis of Massachusetts, to the faulty Massachusetts furlough program and, hence, to the infamous convicted murderer, Willie Horton, who kidnapped and raped a white woman while on furlough. "There is, [after all], no stronger metaphor for racial hatred in our country than the black man raping the white woman."[83]

In 1992, Bill Clinton proved that Republicans were not the only ones who could effectively use the politics of race to reinvigorate a campaign and win an election. Clinton used the wedge issues of race on more than one occasion to revive his struggling campaign.[84] His single most significant opportunity presented itself when Jesse Jackson's Rainbow Coalition gave a forum to Sister Souljah, a little-known rap star who seemed to have voiced her approval of blacks attacking innocent whites during the Los Angeles riots of 1992. After Bill Clinton publicly criticized Jesse Jackson and the Rainbow Coalition for inviting the radical entertainer to speak, "his approval rating among white voters immediately soared."[85] He went on to win the presidency and serve two terms in office.

## Summary

Media-based black-male bashing, however, did not end in 1992. It continues today (again, motivated more by political and economic expediency than by racism), even as we usher in the historic administration of President Barack Obama. Several studies suggest that, not unlike the mass media of the previous two centuries, much of the information we gain from the twenty-first century mass media pertaining to race results in the reinforcement of old racial stereotypes that feed preexisting perceptions of black people.[86] For example, Mary Beth Oliver et al. (2004) and Travis L. Dixon (2008) each concluded from *current* research that media presentations as ordinary as the television network news can be viewed as a *sociocultural agent* that socializes viewers to associate *black* with negatives like *poverty*, *welfare*, *drugs*, *crime*, and *violence*.[87] In no uncertain terms, media-based black-male bashing, in whatever form, has been a part of the American experience for more than three hundred years, and there is absolutely no sign of its dissipation. Our black boys and their forefathers have been caught up in a never-ending cycle of public disparagement and debasement that has significantly influenced how they are viewed by the nation in general and by impressionable children in particular. As Clint C. Wilson II and Felix Gutierrez stated in *Race, Multiculturalism, and the Media* (1995), "The images presented by the media are often the first impressions [children] have of a group or topic and parents or other adults are not always present to help [them] understand what the media are presenting," making them vulnerable to the residual effects of media images and portrayals.[88] Our children are obviously our future, and as their belief system goes, so goes that of the nation.

# Conclusion:
## Why Our Black Boys Choose Enslavement

*All of our experiences fuse into our personality. Everything that has ever happened to us is an ingredient.*

—Malcolm X

At this point, it should be abundantly clear that the life choices made by many of our sons and brothers are almost certainly negatively influenced by the four basic agencies of socialization: (1) the family of orientation, (2) the school system, (3) the peer group, and (4) the mass media. How else can one explain why so many *normal* (at birth) black and brown children have such disproportionate *abnormal* outcomes? If our pants-sagging, crotch-holding, hyperaggressive black boys—who describe themselves as *niggas*—represent the fruit of our labor, would it not stand to reason that there is something severely wrong with the tree from which they came? According to the Office of Juvenile Justice and Delinquency Prevention (2007), for thirty years now, black juveniles have outpaced their white, Hispanic, and Asian counterparts by a margin of more than 2 to 1 in the commission of murders, aggravated assaults, weapons law violations, forcible rapes, robberies, and motor vehicle thefts.[1] The U.S. Department of Justice (2008) has even estimated (based on current rates of first incarceration) that approximately 32 percent of black males will enter state or federal prison during their lifetime, compared to 17 percent of Hispanic males and 6 percent of white males.[2] So, the overarching question continues to be: *why* do so many of our black boys *choose* enslavement? That is, what role do the four agencies of socialization play in the creation and exacerbation of debilitating pathologies or personality flaws that make our children more prone to choosing the path of incarceration through criminality?

In this concluding section, I not only intend to show that life-altering pathologies, like (1) despising one's own "blackness," (2) lacking self-confidence, (3) being fixated on immediate satisfaction, (4) having a warped sense of manhood, and (5) harboring a deep hatred and paranoia of white people, are self-evident among too many of our black boys, but also that the fingerprints of the family, the school system, the peer group, and the mass media can be found throughout the proverbial crime scene.

## Despising Their Own Blackness

Skin color is certainly not the total depth and breadth of who we are as complex human beings. At the same time, however, when one lives in a country where race has been so historically significant, its meaning obviously goes well beyond the simplicity of mere pigmentation. Our skin color is, after all, the cloak or *the veil* (a concept popularized by the prominent black sociologist W. E. B. Du Bois) that we are destined to wear throughout our lives. It is one of the most essential nonverbal clues (along with facial features and hair type) to heritage, culture, and possible personality traits. This reality represents a positive human condition for some and a negative one for others. Our black boys, in particular, have been donned with a veil that many of them have *learned* to despise because it is decorated with so many negatives. And to despise even a part of one's self is tantamount to self-hatred. Why is it that black-on-black violence is still one of America's biggest—albeit underreported—social problems in this first decade of the twenty-first century? Why is it that as recently as 2005, 80 percent of all nonfatal violent crimes and 93 percent of all homicides committed against blacks, were committed by black offenders?[3] Is this a demonstration of a devaluation of "blackness"? Is this evidence of self-hatred?

Professors Ronald E. Hall and Jesenia M. Pizarro (2008) suggest that self-hate has become so ingrained in the black male psyche that "the black community, [itself], has come to tolerate 'black-on-black' crime, especially black male homicides, as a normal course of daily events."[4] Black males, according to Hall and Pizarro, are unique among social groups in their level of pathogenic disregard for their racial peers.[5] And many scholars have made the connection between expressions of hatred toward one's racial group and feelings of hatred toward "self."[6] One of the most-cited promoters of the black self-hatred thesis was psychologist Dr. Kenneth B. Clark (whose findings were heavily referenced in the 1954 *Brown v. Board of Education* Supreme Court case) who, along with his wife, Dr. Mamie Clark, conducted a series of extensive studies between 1939 and the early 1950s on white and black children in the North and the South. From their famous doll-preference experiments, the Clarks drew the same conclusion in the 1940s and 1950s that many social scientists (e.g., Dr. Alvin F. Poussaint, Dr. Michael Eric Dyson, and Dr. Cornel West) have drawn since: self-hatred is running rampant amongst our black boys.

In the early twentieth century, two standard-bearers of sociology, Charles Horton Cooley (1902) and George Herbert Mead (1934), developed the insight that the *self-concept* (the image you eventually have of yourself) is a direct product of a child's exposure to *symbols* (e.g., words, gestures, attitudes, behaviors, and images) produced by significant agents or agencies of socialization.[7] Accordingly, our young black males, many of whom have been diseased with a severe disdain for their own "blackness," had to have been infected by the blatantly negative symbols of obviously corrupted agencies of socialization. These negative symbols have, cumulatively, created a definition of "blackness" that has instilled shame and subsequent self-hatred in the minds of our black boys. And the first and primary contributor to this self-destructive self-concept is the titular head of the black family—the uninvolved, absentee father. He teaches his sons in absentia that "blackness" is synonymous with laziness, indifference, and irresponsible behavior. He makes them feel as if they were fundamentally flawed in some way and that fatherlessness is a natural state for black children. And he leaves the mother to fend for herself (financially and emotionally) as she unwittingly socializes her boys to associate black masculinity with "long shots," like sports or entertainment, and black femininity with academic achievement and success.

The school system continues the ruinous work of the disorganized black family by offering black male students very few role models in the classroom; by reinforcing, through low expectations, the notion that the black intellect is inferior to that of other groups; and by making black males the "poster boys" of special education programs.

But the degrading symbols of "blackness" do not stop there. Within their own peer group, our black boys have championed the old racial stereotypes, making stupidity, laziness, aggressiveness, and hypersexuality a large part of their collective identity. To be "down" with the "brothers" is to "act out" these negative racial stereotypes and accept the perpetually derogatory label of *nigger* (in the form of *nigga*) as a reward.

The mass media, of course, supports this unenviable image of "blackness" by maintaining its three-hundred-year display of the criminalized, sex-crazed, lazy buffoon in many television news stories; in movies created by black and white filmmakers; in books, magazines, and newspaper columns; and in a host of other media. It is no wonder that our black boys despise their God-given dark veil and harbor the lowest self-esteem of any social group.

## Lacking in Self-Confidence

The *Encyclopedia of Human Behavior* (1994) defines *self-esteem* as "the evaluative dimension of self-knowledge, referring to how a person appraises himself or herself."[8] In other words, *self-esteem* is a reflection of the value we place on ourselves based on others' responses to us and based on our perceived inadequacies, capabilities, and accomplishments that we present to the world. Because many young black males are saturated with self-hatred, their low self-esteem and, hence, their weak sense of *self-efficacy* (another word for *self-confidence*) are simply par for the course.

According to the *Encyclopedia of Psychology, self-efficacy* is the degree to which a person believes in their capacity to perform in ways that give them control over events that affect their lives. Current literature is replete with evidence of a severe lack of self-efficacy or self-confidence among our black boys, particularly in the area of academic achievement. Larry E. Davis (2003), a professor and director of the Center on Race and Social Problems at the University of Pittsburgh, conducted a five-year study of race and gender disparities in educational outcomes and levels of self-esteem and self-confidence, using a large student sample from a nationally representative inner city, predominantly black high school. Davis found that although *global* (general) self-confidence was not lacking among black male students, *domain-specific* (e.g., academic) self-confidence most certainly was. Black boys in Davis' study "thought themselves less capable academically and [thus felt less] confident about their ability to read and write and do schoolwork."[9]

Even elite black college students experience lowered self-confidence when placed in direct academic competition with their white counterparts of similar abilities. In *Thin Ice* (1999), social psychologist Claude M. Steele framed this syndrome as *stereotype threat*. He and his colleagues found that when their test group of high-achieving black and white sophomores from Stanford University were placed in a high pressure test-taking environment where intellectual ability was believed to be the primary focus, white students, on average, outperformed black students, even when they were evenly matched by incoming SAT scores.[10] Steele's experiment has been replicated several times since his 1999 study was published, and the same or similar results were produced.[11]

At the very least, some semblance of domain-specific self-confidence (whether academic, vocational, or otherwise) is essential to personality—if only for the small incremental progressions that are a natural part of survival. In fact, a person's level of domain-specific self-confidence can be said to be in direct correlation with his or her potential level of success in life. And yet, too many of our black boys have been found lacking, as they exhibit the all-too-typical signs: (1) general underachievement; (2) avoidance of challenges; (3) anxiety about success; (4) self-defeating excuse-making; and (5) a blind obsession with noncerebral, *seemingly* easy ways of achieving the American dream, like sports or entertainment.

But why does this personality flaw (i.e., lacking self-confidence) reign so prominently among black youths? The answer, of course, lies with the source: the four agencies of socialization. The family, in particular, is especially culpable in this case because, as George Herbert Mead (1934) contends, a child's *basic* self-concept begins to take shape at least by the age of six;[12] and although the processes of socialization and personality development continue well beyond these first few years, global and domain-specific self-confidence are forever affected by this early formation of the self-concept. As such, due to the absence and noninvolvement of their biological father, the economically and emotionally weakened position of their single mother, and the inaccessibility of positive black male role models in their community, the formative years (ages 0 to 6) of our black boys have been left hanging in the balance. Their *basic* self-concept and, hence, their self-confidence, have been sabotaged. How can an absentee father, a frustrated mother, and an unsupportive community provide the level of *socioemotional maintenance* (the love, support, positive feedback, and encouragement that a child requires for proper development) needed to create a healthy, self-confidence-promoting self-concept in the mind of the black male child? And how can we reasonably expect any child to genuinely pursue a "legitimate" long-term goal without the necessary self-confidence to believe that he or she will actually achieve that goal? Should we demand from "socially defective" children what we demand from so-called "normal" children? A sense of community responsibility dictates that we answer in the affirmative. But should we then expect similar responses to such demands from the defective and the normal? Common sense tells us that we should not.

## Fixated on Immediate Satisfaction

For example, as we established in chapter one, The Influence of the Family, our black boys have a very strong fixation on immediate satisfaction to the detriment of long-term success. They have not been effectively taught how to delay gratification. They are essentially devoid of a skill that is not only a prerequisite to ultimate career success in adulthood, but also one that has a significant effect on emotional stability, social skill attainment, cognitive ability, and academic achievement. In the *Handbook of Self-Regulation* (2004), Kathleen D. Vohs and Roy F. Baumeister define *self-regulation* or delaying gratification as the processes by which people are able to exercise control over their emotions, impulses or appetites, and task performances for the benefit of some future reward.[13] In addition, according to Joan E. LeFebvre (2003), the ability to delay gratification is a learned skill that begins to emerge between the ages of three and four, and it is essential in the lives of children, adolescents, and adults.[14]

The ability to resist immediate satisfaction, then, becomes an indispensable part of the healthy personality. And to be fixated on immediate satisfaction is to reserve no place for self-control. Young black males are reported by parents, teachers, and law enforcement agencies as being unnaturally aggressive.[15] They participate in more fights at school and are suspended more often for violent offenses than other students.[16] They commit more murders, forcible rapes, robberies, and aggravated assaults per capita than any other social group.[17] They have more children out of wedlock than their white and Asian counterparts combined. And their STD rates (including HIV and AIDS) are the highest in the nation.[18]

These trite but poignant facts are symptomatic of a group of people who have absolutely no belief in *fate control*. Most of our black boys live only for the present because, in their minds, the present is all that they have. Why would anyone with a negative self-image and low self-confidence be interested in delaying gratification or exercising self-control? Even more to the point, *how* can anyone with such deficiencies utilize a skill (self-regulation) that, by definition, cannot be utilized effectively when such deficiencies exist? Our black youths crave immediate satisfaction because their ability to delay gratification has been sabotaged by the four agencies of socialization—especially the family.

In any family, regardless of race or family structure, it is primarily the mother who instills in the children the value of self-regulation or delaying gratification. Even if she works full time outside the home, she still spends more time actively interacting with the children and is, therefore, more involved in child rearing than the father. However, in the single-parent family where the father is absent and unsupportive, the mother's role is irrevocably weakened due to inadequate financial and social capital. She finds herself overwhelmed and frustrated by her insurmountable responsibilities, making her less able to properly socialize her children. The noninvolvement of the father also has a direct deleterious influence on the two primary prerequisites to attaining the skill of self-regulation: a positive self-concept and a high self-esteem.

This is the plight of our black boys, who are overwhelmingly reared (60 percent of them) in fatherless households. And to make matters worse, the school system, the peer group, and the mass media simply exacerbate the failings of the disorganized black family. The school system, for example, by virtue of its overabundance of white female teachers (representing the lion's share of the public school system's accessible adult role models), has inadvertently painted a picture of success—success being the ultimate purpose of delaying gratification—using a white female face—an image that black male students cannot relate to or gain life lessons from.

The black male peer group has also made it difficult for our children to resist immediate satisfaction as it idolizes a category of people who are led and guided by a philosophy of severe impatience, overindulgence, extreme aggressiveness, and "power through criminality"—convicted criminals and ex-cons. And the mass media has glamorized and reinforced this philosophy in movies like *Penitentiary* (1979), *Scarface* (1983), *The Big Score* (1983), *Boyz N the Hood* (1991), *Juice* (1992), *Menace II Society* (1993), *Original Gangsters* (1996), and *Full Clip* (2004). Through a botched socialization process, therefore, our black boys have developed the mindset that hard work and delaying gratification can never measure up to immediate satisfaction and the "coolness" of criminality.

## Having a Warped Sense of Manhood

This goes a long way toward explaining the warped sense of manhood that exists in the black community. But warped as compared to what standard? It is well-known that manhood is not an innate quality residing in the biological composition of the human male. It is not the result of androgens or the possession of a penis.[19] Manhood, in fact, "means different things at different times to different people."[20] It is a social construct that is certainly influenced by culture, generational differences, and perhaps even by certain demographic variables. Having said that, however, there still must be some cross-cultural, intergenerational agreement on the *basic* components of what it means to be a man. Even many of our own historically prominent black leaders, such as Booker T. Washington, W. E. B. DuBois, Marcus Garvey, Martin Luther King, Jr., and Malcolm X, offered differing definitions of masculinity and varying prescriptions for achieving it. But they all seemed to agree that, at the very least, black manhood should be grounded in racial pride, leadership, morality, spirituality, and the patriarchal gender roles of father as leader, provider, and protector.[21]

It is against this timeless standard that we measure our black boys' notion of manhood—a notion forged by fatherlessness, social disorientation, and desperation. As Harvard University professor Orlando Patterson (2006) suggested, many black boys, in their blind, vulnerable state, have turned to the most aggressive members of their peer group as father substitutes, defining their manhood by an almost exaggerated masculinity.[22] They use the behavior of convicted criminals and boisterous neighborhood ex-cons as a litmus test for their own behavior and that of their peers. They have come to view incarceration as the ultimate bar mitzvah for "brothers." In other words, the professional criminal, who defines himself by his own deviance, has become *the* symbol of manhood for our black boys. In *The Black Male Handbook* (2008), Byron Hurt makes it clear that diplomacy does not exist in black male peer relations. And any attempt to use diplomacy as an alternative to physical confrontation, says Hurt, means, in essence, "that you [are] 'a soft nigga', which [is] about the worst thing you could ever be considered among black males."[23] If this is not demonstrative of a warped standard of manhood, especially juxtaposed to the general philosophy of many of our greatest leaders, then how else should it be characterized? Is there any other way to describe a state of manhood born of illegitimacy, rebellion, and rejection?

The black male peer group, whose members are predominantly products of mother-only families, has stepped into the immeasurable void left by the father, providing its own destructive remedy for the absence of an adequately socialized definition of manhood. A mother can teach her sons many things, including *certain* elements of masculinity, but *true* manhood—that which becomes a permanent, irreducible part of the male psyche through active, positive male role modeling—can only be taught by a man. As Jawanza Kunjufu alludes to in *Countering the Conspiracy to Destroy Black Boys* (1985), a single mother's level of success in raising her sons to be *real men* depends on how proactive she is in exposing them to positive male role models and mentors.[24] In other words, according to Kunjufu, "until [black] women admit that only men can make boys into men, and [black] men become responsible for giving direction to at least one male child," the destruction of black boys will continue unabated.[25]

Some may perceive this kind of statement as an attack on the black woman's ability as mother. Yet, it is not her ability as mother that is in question. It is her inability as father that is of consequence. The fact is, a single mother *can* raise her sons to be responsible, well-adjusted, positive-minded men without a man in *her* life. However, she *cannot* raise her sons to be responsible, well-adjusted, positive-minded men without a man in *their* lives. That man can take the form of a positive, caring, involved biological father, stepfather, coach, teacher, boy scout leader, or otherwise. And, optimally, he should belong to the same racial or ethnic group.

So, is there any question as to how our black boys are faring in light of these realities? The majority of their biological fathers are unavailable, "suitable" surrogate fathers and mentors from their extended families and communities are virtually inaccessible, and black male educators in the public school system are almost nonexistent. This leaves only the exacerbating influences of the dysfunctional black male peer group, the stereotype-perpetuating mass media, and the well-meaning but ill-informed black single mother who unwittingly teaches her sons that manhood is less about academic achievement and personal responsibility, and more about seeking unattainable goals and fighting a level of racism that no longer exists.

## Harboring Hatred and Paranoia of White People

This brand of socialization may partially explain why so many black Americans view racism, in particular, not as a scourge on the wane, nor even as an influence that has plateaued since the 1970s, but as a constantly growing force that is more subtle (less recognizable) and insidious than the racism of the past. A recent *USA Today*/Gallup poll (2008) seems to bear out this assertion. Using a national sample of 1,935 American adults (600 blacks, 500 Hispanics, and 835 whites), *USA Today* and Gallup found that 78 percent of blacks feel that racism against them is widespread, while only 59 percent of Hispanics and 51 percent of whites feel that racism against blacks is widespread. In addition, they found that the vast majority of blacks (57 to 80 percent) also feel that racial discrimination is a major factor in their educational levels, income levels, prison rates, and even in their average life expectancy. But, strikingly, less than 55 percent of Hispanics and less than 45 percent of whites feel that racial discrimination against blacks is a major factor in these outcome categories.[26]

Based on this and other polls and studies,[27] it appears that blacks are determined to maintain their status as victims, which infers that there must be a victimizer. There must be an object of blame, an oppressor, a precipitator of all black social ills. Such a persona would certainly generate paranoia and justifiable hatred. In the minds of our black boys, the dated concept of "The Man" (a white perpetrator who searches for and seizes upon any opportunity to inflict on blacks some sort of social damage) is still a part of the American landscape. To them, their feelings of hatred and paranoia are well-founded. They have been socialized to believe that a former enemy—"the racist white man"—is still as strong, ubiquitous, and influential as he once was. The world of the past has been pulled over the eyes of our black male children, blinding them to the truth, crippling them with anxiety, fear, and insecurity. They have been prepared for a world that no longer exists, while they are systematically destroyed in the world that does. Our black boys have, essentially, joined the *Cult of Victimology*, where racism is used as a crutch, and where hatred and paranoia have become psychological distractions in the midst of failure, a lack of effort, and criminality.

As already said, the black single mother unwittingly promotes these debilitating feelings of hatred and paranoia (directed toward white people) in the minds of her sons by teaching them to anticipate an unrealistic level of race-based prejudice and maltreatment in her well-meaning attempt to shield them from the discrimination that she perceives they will one day surely confront. But the burden of blame does not rest solely on the shoulders of the black single mother. The white female teacher, the black male peer group, and the mass media each play their own part in reinforcing our black boys' psychosis and further justifying their feelings of hatred and paranoia. White female teachers, who control the fate of 65 percent of America's classrooms, have made significant contributions to our nation's children. However, even those with "hearts of gold," who have the best of intentions, irrespective of racial differences, enter the classroom with perceptions (based on their own pre-socialized identity orientations) of their students that are filtered through a prism of white dominance, social privilege, and lingering racial stereotypes, resulting in lowered expectations of their black male students which, to these students, feels like racism.

The black male peer group reacts to the lessons taught by the school system (the white female teacher) and the family (the black single mother) by simply rejecting all things considered white. In other words, our black boys demonstrate their disdain and distrust of white people by acting out racism-born stereotypes (an ironic, peculiar fact) that are diametrically opposed to what they view as the constructs of "whiteness": intelligent, hardworking, mild-mannered, and sexually responsible. As such, stupidity, laziness, aggressiveness, and hypersexuality have become the collective identity of the black male peer group. And to add fuel to the fire of paranoia, black males, young and old, rarely see themselves portrayed in a positive light by the mass media. With the exception of particular movies, selected sitcoms, and isolated human interest stories, most newspapers, magazines, television programs and major films consistently associate *black* with negatives like *poverty*, *welfare*, *drugs*, *crime*, and *violence* to a degree that is inconsistent with reality. Our black boys have been caught up in a never-ending cycle of public disparagement and debasement that has significantly influenced how they are viewed by white people, and how white people are viewed by them: as objects of hatred.

## Summary

In 1992, when this author was a student at the Albany campus of State University of New York, I had a poignant, albeit purely anecdotal, experience that gave me some insight about the racial stereotypes that still lingered in the American mindset. On a beautiful April afternoon just before dusk, as I studied at the small kitchen table in my upstairs apartment in a section of on-campus graduate housing ironically labeled "Freedom Quad," I could hear through my open window a group of white male graduate students in the apartment below, discussing what they called "the black problem." Of the many stereotypical statements I heard that day, one, in particular, has stayed with me for over fifteen years, giving me additional motivation to write this book. The complete comment was as follows: "Believe me, those people love prison. It's a nigger's paradise" [followed by group laughter].

I remember, in the midst of my anger, trying to rationalize the absurdity of that statement with the fact that so many blacks were, in fact, in prison, in jail (over 660,000 were in jail or prison in 1993, representing about 48 percent of the total incarcerated population),[28] or on parole. But even still, how could *anyone* love prison? As mostly violent repeat offenders, the majority of the one million blacks imprisoned today are housed in either medium or maximum security facilities. Life for them is no "crystal stair."

Typically, an inmate's day begins between 5 AM and 6 AM. They are given about forty-five minutes to take their semiweekly shower, clean their living areas, get dressed, and make their beds. They are then escorted to the dining hall in shifts and are allowed thirty minutes to eat breakfast. No later than 7 AM, all inmates are assembled, counted, searched, and given their work assignments for that day. Depending upon individual risk, they may be required to work inside the prison itself or at a designated community work site directly supervised by correctional officers. They work from approximately 8 AM until 2 PM, receiving several scheduled rest breaks and one thirty-minute lunch break. After their work assignments are complete, they are, again, assembled, counted, and searched before they are given permission to spend their "daily hour" on the prison yard or in an outside cage. They eat supper at 5 PM and are given until 7 PM to participate in pre-chosen programs, such as religious services or narcotics anonymous classes. Inmates return to their dorms or cell blocks by 8 PM, where they undergo a final headcount and are locked down for the remainder of the evening. "Lights out" is normally at about 11 PM. This schedule is essentially repeated day after day, week after week, year after year. No sane person could love this life. So, why do our black boys choose enslavement? Why do they have such an irrational attachment to the penal slave system? Why do so many of them choose incarceration through criminality?

Perhaps the best way to answer these questions is with a question: if a person was a product of a uniquely destructive socialization process that built within him a sense of self-hatred, low self-confidence, an inability to delay gratification, a warped standard of manhood, and a deep disdain and paranoia of white people, would that person be more prone to choosing life, liberty, responsibility, and success; or failure, criminality, prison, and death?

If the answer is still elusive, consider what the fields of psychology and social psychology tell us. The *Encyclopedia of Psychology* reminds us that self-hatred (e.g., despising one's own "blackness") and low self-confidence not only have a suppressive effect on a child's ability to delay gratification, but they are also key determinants in the development of low self-esteem.[29] And, according to *The Blackwell Encyclopedia of Social Psychology* (1996), low self-esteem is directly responsible for many negatives: (1) a poorly articulated, uncertain, and internally inconsistent self-concept; (2) a high value being placed on personal negative attributes; (3) large discrepancies existing between the actual self-conception (what one believes is true of the self) and the ideal (desired or hoped for) self; (4) a greater vulnerability to psychological disorders, such as depression and despair; (5) a tendency toward anxiety, avoidance of risk, and self-sabotage; (6) negative expectations of future outcomes, leading to bad decision-making and poor life choices; and (7) less overall happiness and satisfaction.[30] Furthermore, when one develops an exaggerated, hyperaggressive masculinity in the absence of a legitimately socialized definition of manhood from a "suitable" father figure, one tends to become desensitized to violence and criminality and guided by aggressiveness. If we then add an unjustified fear of racism and a paranoia of white people to this already damaged personality, it becomes crystal clear as to why so many of our black boys choose enslavement. They have been left psychologically damaged and broken by the four basic agencies of socialization: the family, the school system, the peer group, and the mass media. And many of the choices they make are precipitated by feelings of hopelessness and despair emanating from pathologies (discussed previously) created, induced, and perpetuated by a botched socialization process.

These statements, however, are not meant to grant absolution to black males or free them of personal and social responsibility. Because, as mentioned earlier, there are many examples of those who have endured severely negative circumstances and still made positive life choices despite the odds. Jesse Jackson was born out of wedlock to a poor teenage mother and to an uncaring father who lived on the same street with his own family, yet had no time for his illegitimate son. Jesse was also rejected by his own community because of the circumstances of his birth, as he was constantly referred to as "that bastard child." Oprah Winfrey was also born to a poor, unwed teenage mother; and between the ages of nine and thirteen, Oprah was raped by a cousin, molested by a family friend, and sexually abused by an uncle. As a consequence of that mistreatment, she became severely rebellious and promiscuous and eventually became pregnant and gave birth to a stillborn baby at the age of fourteen. Tyler Perry suffered years of abuse at the hands of his alcoholic father, who would sometimes beat him with an extension cord until the skin was peeling off his back. He was also seduced by a friend's mother at the age of ten, molested by another friend's father shortly thereafter, and he soon discovered that his own father was molesting a neighborhood girl. Maya Angelou was molested by her mother's boyfriend at the age of seven and was too ashamed to confide in anyone but her brother. When she later learned that an uncle had killed her attacker, she felt that her words had killed the man, causing her to fall silent for five years. She would not speak again until she was thirteen. Malcolm X not only experienced pervasive poverty and a perpetually violent household, but he also endured the malicious burning of his home (by the white supremacist organization Black Legion) when he was four, the murder of his father when he was six, the emotional breakdown and committal of his mother to a mental institution when he was twelve, and the pronouncement by one of his favorite teachers (a white English teacher) that becoming a lawyer was not a "realistic goal for a nigger," when he was fourteen.

These powerful examples of great people emerging from the bleakest circumstances show that even in the face of what can certainly be categorized as *hopelessness* and *despair*, choice—as difficult as it may be—is always a factor.

# Notes

### Introduction: The Plantation of Choice

1. A reference made by a group of white graduate students (1992) on the Albany campus of State University of New York, overheard by this author while residing in a section of the university's graduate housing ironically labeled "Freedom Quad." The complete comment was as follows: "Believe me, those people love prison. It's a nigger's paradise" [followed by group laughter]. This recollection is anecdotal at best, but still poignant, nevertheless.

2. Belinda Hurmence, ed., *Before Freedom: 48 Oral Histories of Former North and South Carolina Slaves* (Winston Salem, NC: John F. Blair, Publisher, 1990), 20–21.

3. Ibid., 42.

4. Ibid., 74–75.

5. Ibid., 46–51.

6. Ibid., xi–xii.

7. Ibid., xi–xii.

8. Michael Eric Dyson, *The Michael Eric Dyson Reader* (New York: Basic Civitas Books, 2004), 223.

9. National Organization of Hispanics in Criminal Justice, *Census: More Blacks, Latinos Live in Cells than in Dorms*

(Kissimmee, FL: NOHCJ, 2006); U.S. Bureau of the Census, *Minority Population Tops 100 Million* (Washington, DC: GPO, 2007); U.S. Department of Justice, *Prison Statistics* (Washington DC: GPO, 2008).

10. Ibid.

11. Ibid.

12. *Favorite Poems of Henry Wadsworth Longfellow* (Garden City, NY: Doubleday & Company, 1967), 108–109.

13. John W. Blassingame, John R. McKivigan, and Peter P. Hinks, eds., *Narrative of the Life of Frederick Douglass* (New Haven & London: Yale University Press, 2001), 35–36.

14. James O. Horton and Lois E. Horton, *Slavery and the Making of America* (New York: Oxford University Press, 2005), 30–33.

15. The Mariners' Museum, "Captive Passage: The Transatlantic Slave Trade and the Making of the Americas," The Mariners' Museum, http://www.mariner.org/captive passage/introduction/int001.html (accessed January 19, 2008).

16. Richard Hooker, ed., L.W. King, trans., "Mesopotamia: The Code of Hammurabi," http://www.wsu.edu/~dee/MESO/CODE.HTM (accessed January 20, 2008).

17. O. R. Gurney, *The Hittites* (Baltimore: Penguin, 1954), 71.

18. Barbara Solow, ed., *Slavery and the Rise of the Atlantic System* (New York: Cambridge University Press, 1994), 18; P. C. Emmer, "The Dutch and the Making of the Second Atlantic System," in *Slavery and the Rise of the Atlantic System*, ed. Barbara Solow (New York: Cambridge University Press, 1994), 95; John Kelly Thornton, *Africa and Africans in the Making of the Atlantic*

*World, 1400–1800*, 2nd ed. (New York: Cambridge University Press, 1998), 94–95.

19. Kevin Bales, *New Slavery: A Reference Handbook* (Santa Barbara, CA: ABC-CLIO, 2000), 5–6.

20. Ibid., 6.

21. Ibid., 3.

22. *The American Heritage College Dictionary*, 4th ed., s.vv. "slave," "Slav."

23. *Encyclopaedia Britannica Online*, s.v. "slavery," http:// www.britannica.com/EBchecked/topic/548305/slavery(accessed May 23, 2009).

24. *A Dictionary of the Social Sciences* (New York: The Free Press, 1964), s.v. "slavery."

25. Bales, *New Slavery*, 3.

26. Howard Dodson, "How Slavery Helped Build a World Economy," *National Geographic News*, February 2003, http:// news.nationalgeographic.com/news/2003/01/0131_030203 _jubilee2.html (accessed January 31, 2008).

27. *The American Heritage Dictionary*, rev. ed., s.v. "confine."

28. Jon M. Shepard and Robert W. Greene, *Sociology and You* (Columbus, OH: Glencoe/McGraw-Hill, 2003), 206.

29. Bales, *New Slavery*, 8–10; Trevor Bryce, *Life and Society in the Hittite World* (New York: Oxford University Press, 2002), 52.

30. *Encyclopaedia Britannica Online*, s.v. "slavery," http:// www.britannica.com/EBchecked/topic/548305/slavery(accessed May 23, 2009).

31. *Webster's Ninth New Collegiate Dictionary* (Springfield, MA: Merriam-Webster Publishers, 1990), s.v. "prison."

32. James Q. Wilson and John J. DiIulio, Jr., *American Government: Institutions and Policies* (New York: Houghton Mifflin, 2001), A15.

33. Ibid., A13–A15.

34. *Encyclopaedia Britannica Online*, s.v. "prison," http://www.britannica.com/ EBchecked/topic/477205/prison (accessed May 23, 2009).

35. *Encyclopaedia Britannica*, 15th ed., s.v. "Prisons and Penology."

36. Wex Legal Dictionary and Encyclopedia, "Prisoners' Rights," Cornell University Law School—Legal Information Institute, http://www.law.cornell.edu/wex/index.php/Prisoners' _rights (accessed February 29, 2008).

37. *Merriam-Webster Dictionary Online*, s.v. "slave," http://www.merriam-webster.com/dictionary/slave (accessed February 9, 2008); Bales, *New Slavery*, 3.

38. Kimmett Edgar and Tim Newell, *Restorative Justice in Prisons: A Guide to Making it Happen* (Winchester, England: Waterside Press, 2006), 57–58.

39. *Encyclopedia Americana*, rev. ed. (Danbury, CT: Scholastic Library Publishing, 2006), s.v. "prison"; *Encyclopaedia Britannica*, 15th ed., s.v. "prisons and penology."

40. *The American Heritage Dictionary*, rev. ed., s.v. "prisoner."

41. Gwen Smith Ingley, "Inmate Labor: Yesterday, Today and Tomorrow," *Corrections Today* 58, no. 1 (February 1996): 28.

42. Net Industries, "Prisons—Prison Industries: Excellent Idea Or Exploitation," Net Industries, http://social.jrank. org/pages/1348/Prisons-Prison-Industries-Excellent-Idea-or-Exploitation.html (accessed February 27, 2008); Marylee N.

Reynolds, "Back on the Chain Gang," *Corrections Today* 58, no. 2 (April 1996): 183.

43. Insideprison.com, "A Brief History of the Prison Industry," *Insideprison.com*, April 2006, http://www.insideprison.com/prison-industry-labor.asp (accessed April 9, 2008); U.S. Department of Justice, *Federal Prison Industries: The Myths, Successes, and Challenges of One of America's Most Successful Government Programs* (Washington DC: UNICOR, 2003).

44. Oregon Department of Corrections, *Inmate Work Crew Information* (Salem, OR: Operations Division, 2007).

45. U.S. Department of Justice, *Federal Prison Industries: Fiscal Year 2006 Annual Report* (Washington DC: UNICOR, 2006).

46. Iowa Prison Industries, *Annual Report: 2006–2007* (Des Moines: IPI, 2007), 13, 20; Alabama Department of Corrections, *Annual Report: Fiscal Year 2006* (Montgomery: ACI, 2006), 22–23; MINNCOR Industries, *Evaluation Report—Fiscal Year 2009* (St. Paul, MN: Office of the Legislative Auditor, 2009), 21, 26.

47. Kim Gilmore, "Slavery and Prison—Understanding the Connections," *Social Justice* 27, no. 3 (Fall 2000): 200.

48. Ibid., 199–200.

49. Thomas Johnson Michie, Thomas Jefferson, and Peachy Ridgway Grattan, *Virginia Reports: Jefferson—33 Grattan, 1730–1880* (Charlottesville, VA: The Michie Company, 1901), 1026.

50. *Cooper v. Pate*, 378 U.S. 546 (1964).

51. Wex Legal Dictionary and Encyclopedia, "Prisoners' rights," Cornell University Law School—Legal Information Institute, http://www.law.cornell.edu/wex/index.php/Prisoners'_rights (accessed February 29, 2008).

52. The Staff of the *Washington Post, Being a Black Man: At the Corner of Progress and Peril* (New York: Public Affairs Books, 2007), 239.

53. U.S. Department of Justice, *Crime in the United States: Arrests by Race, 2006* (Washington DC: GPO, 2006).

# 1. The Influence of the Family

1. Jon M. Shepard and Robert W. Greene, *Sociology and You* (Columbus, OH: Glencoe/McGraw-Hill, 2003), 121.

2. Gerald Handel, "Revising Socialization Theory," *American Sociological Review* 55, no. 3 (June 1990): 465.

3. Child Trends Data Bank, "Family Structure," Child Trends, http://www.childtrends databank.org/pdf/59_PDF.pdf (accessed May 19, 2008).

4. Andrew Billingsley, *Climbing Jacob's Ladder: The Enduring Legacy of African-American Families* (New York: Simon & Schuster, 1992), 36.

5. Ibid., 36; Child Trends Data Bank, "Family Structure," Child Trends, http://www. childtrendsdatabank.org/pdf/59_PDF.pdf (accessed May 19, 2008).

6. Frank F. Furstenberg, Jr., Theodore Hershberg, and John Modell, "The Origins of the Female-Headed Black Family: The Impact of the Urban Experience," *Journal of Interdisciplinary History* 6, no. 2 (Autumn 1975): 219.

7. Shepard and Greene, *Sociology*, 292–293.

8. William O'Hare, "An Evaluation of Three Theories Regarding the Growth of Black Female-Headed Families," *Journal of Urban Affairs* 10, no. 2 (June 1988): Abstract.

9. Ibid.

10. Richard M. Stana, *State and Federal Prisoners: Profiles of Inmate Characteristics in 1991 and 1997* (Darby, PA: Diane Publishing Company, 2000), 55, 64.

11. E. Franklin Frazier, "Problems and Needs of Negro Children and Youth Resulting from Family Disorganization," *The Journal of Negro Education* 19, no. 3 (Summer 1950): 276–277.

12. Patrick Fagan and Stephanie Coontz, "Q: Are Single-Parent Families a Major Cause of Social Dysfunction?" *Insight on the News*, December 8, 1997.

13. Deborah A. Dawson, "Family Structure and Children's Health and Well-Being: Data from the 1988 National Health Interview Survey on Child Health," *Journal of Marriage and the Family* 53, no. 3 (August 1991): 576.

14. Ibid., 573.

15. Sheila Fitzgerald Krein and Andrea H. Beller, "Educational Attainment of Children from Single-Parent Families: Differences by Exposure, Gender, and Race," *Demography* 25, no. 2 (May 1988): 221.

16. Paul Roberts and Bill Moseley, "Father's Time," *Psychology Today* 29, no. 3 (May/June 1996): 49.

17. Glenn T. Stanton, *How Fathers Matter for Healthy Child Development* (Wheeling, IL: A & M Partnership, 2003).

18. Child Trends Data Bank, "Family Structure," Child Trends, http://www.childtrends databank.org/pdf/59_PDF.pdf (accessed May 19, 2008).

19. M. Eileen Matlack et al., "Family Correlates of Social Skill Deficits in Incarcerated and Nonincarcerated Adolescents," *Adolescence* 29, no. 113 (Spring 1994): 119–128.

20. Nancy Vaden-Kiernan et al., "Household Family Structure and Children's Aggressive Behavior: A Longitudinal Study of Urban Elementary School Children," *Journal of Abnormal Child Psychology* 23, no. 5 (October 1995): 553.

21. Joan E. LeFebvre, *Parenting the Preschooler: Self-Regulation* (Eagle River, WI: University of Wisconsin, Extension, 2003).

22. Ibid.

23. Wendy S. Grolnick and Richard M. Ryan, "Parent Styles Associated with Children's Self-Regulation and Competence in School," *Journal of Educational Psychology* 81, no. 2 (June 1989): 152.

24. Robert Mark Silverman, ed., *Community-Based Organizations: The Intersection of Social Capital and Local Context in Contemporary Urban Society* (Detroit, MI: Wayne State University Press, 2004), 21–22.

25. Shepard and Greene, *Sociology*, 348.

26. Bruce Robert Hare and Louis A. Castenell, Jr., "No Place to Run, No Place to Hide: Comparative Status and Future Prospects of Black Boys," in *Beginnings: The Social and Affective Development of Black Children*, eds. Margaret Beale Spencer, Geraldine Kearse Brookins, and Walter Recharde Allen (Hillsdale, NJ: Lawrence Erlbaum Associates, 1985), 209; Cassandra George Sturges, "Do Black Mothers Exploit Their Sons?" Socyberty, March 27, 2007, http://www.socyberty.com/Ethnicity/Do-Black-Mothers-Exploit-Their-Sons.19464 (accessed July 5, 2008).

27. Ellis Cose, "The Black Gender Gap," *Newsweek*, March 3, 2003; Hare and Castenell, Jr., "No Place to Run," 209.

28. Shepard and Greene, *Sociology*, 513; Bruce Banter, "Hip Hop Mathematics: A Lesson for Teachers," Playahata.

com, August 2005, http://www.playahata.com/pages/banner/ hiphopmathematics.htm (accessed July 8, 2008).

29. Cose, "Gender Gap."

30. Susan Tifft, "Fighting the Failure Syndrome," *Time*, May 21, 1990.

31. Leon D. Caldwell and Le'Roy Reese, "The Fatherless Father: On Becoming Dad," in *Black Fathers: An Invisible Presence in America*, eds. Michael E. Connor and Joseph L. White (Mahwah, NJ: Lawrence Erlbaum Associates, 2006), 170; Leon D. Caldwell and Joseph L. White, "Generative Fathering: Challenges to Black Masculinity and Identity," in *Black Fathers*, Connor and White, 61; Sarah Allen and Kerry Daly, *The Effects of Father Involvement: An Updated Research Summary of the Evidence* (Guelph, ON: FIRA-CURA, 2007), 17–19.

32. Charles Whitaker, "Do Black Males Need Special Schools?" *Ebony*, March 1991; Jet Staff, "Is It More Difficult to Raise Girls or Boys?" *Jet*, December 6, 1999.

33. Whitaker, "Special Schools?"

34. National Fatherhood Initiative, "Father Friendly Check-Up for Parents as Teachers," Fatherhood.org, https://www.fatherhood.org/BeginSurvey4.asp?sid=5 (accessed July 21, 2008).

35. Elaine Sorensen and Chava Zibman, "Poor Dads Who Don't Pay Child Support: Deadbeats or Disadvantaged?" *Urban Institute*, no. B-30 (April 2001): 1.

36. William Julius Wilson, "The Woes of the Inner-City African American Father," in *Black Fathers in Contemporary American Society: Strengths, Weaknesses, and Strategies for Change*, eds. Obie Clayton, Ronald B. Mincy, and David Blankenhorn (New York: Russell Sage Foundation, 2003), 9; Naomi Gerstel

and Natalia Sarkistan, "Sociological Perspectives on Families and Work: The Impact of Gender, Class, and Race," in *The Work and Family Handbook: Multi-Disciplinary Perspectives and Approaches*, eds. Marcie Pitt-Catsouphes, Ellen Ernst Kossek, and Stephen Sweet (Mahwah, NJ: Lawrence Erlbaum Associates, 2006), 251; Jonathan N. Livingston and John L. McAdoo, "The Roles of African American Fathers in the Socialization of Their Children," in *Black Families*, 4th ed., ed. Harriette Pipes McAdoo (Thousand Oaks, CA: Sage Publications, Inc., 2007), 220–221.

37. Ronald B. Mincy and Hillard Pouncy, "The Marriage Mystery: Marriage, Assets, and the Expectations of African American Families," in *Black* Fathers, Clayton, Mincy, and Blankenhorn, 51; Caldwell and Reese, "On Becoming Dad," in *Black Fathers*, Connor and White, 171–172; Whitaker, "Special Schools?"

38. Naomi Gerstel and Natalia Sarkistan, "Sociological Perspectives on Families and Work: The Impact of Gender, Class, and Race," in *The Work and Family Handbook*, Pitt-Catsouphes, Kossek, and Sweet, 251; Livingston and McAdoo, "The Roles of African American Fathers," in *Black Families*, 228.

39. Caldwell and White, "Generative Fathering," in *Black Fathers*, 56.

40. Mark Roth, "Sociologist Suggests Ways to Get Fathers More Involved with Kids," *Pittsburgh Post-Gazette*, April 6, 2006; E. Bernard Franklin, "African-American Boys: The Cries of a Crisis," *Kansas City Star*, January 28, 2006.

41. Roth, "Sociologist Suggests."

42. CNN Staff, "Poll: Most Americans See Lingering Racism—In Others," Cable News Network, December 12,

2006, http://www.cnn.com/2006/US/12/12/racism.poll/index.html (accessed August 4, 2008).

43. Maldwyn A. Jones, *The Limits of Liberty: American History 1607–1980* (New York: Oxford University Press, 1991), 267–270.

44. Ibid., 272–273.

45. Jeffrey S. Adler, "Introduction," in *African-American Mayors: Race, Politics, and the American City*, eds. David R. Colburn and Jeffrey S. Adler (Chicago: University of Illinois Press, 2001), 1.

46. David R. Colburn, "Running for Office: African-American Mayors from 1967 to 1996," in *African-American Mayors*, 24–26.

47. Jones, *The Limits of Liberty*, 581.

48. Ibid.

49. Ibid.

50. Richard L. Morrill and O. Fred Donaldson, "Geographical Perspectives on the History of Black America," *Economic Geography* 48, no. 1 (January 1972): 19–20.

51. Jones, *The Limits of Liberty*, 536.

52. Morrill and Donaldson, "Geographical Perspectives": 20.

53. Jones, *The Limits of Liberty*, 554.

54. Martin Luther King, Jr., speech in Memphis, Tennessee, April 3, 1968, in *Martin Luther King, Jr.: A Documentary ... Montgomery to Memphis*, ed. Flip Schulke (New York: Norton, 1976), 224.

55. Juan Williams, *Enough: The Phony Leaders, Dead-End Movements, and Culture of Failure that are Undermining Black*

*America—and What We Can Do about It* (New York: Three Rivers Press, 2006), 220.

56. John McWhorter, *Losing the Race: Self-Sabotage in Black America* (New York: Harper Collins, 2001), xi.

57. Shelby Steele, *The Content of Our Character: A New Vision of Race in America* (New York: St. Martin's Press, 1990), 28.

58. McWhorter, *Losing the Race*, 43.

## 2. The Influence of the School System

1. Beverly Daniel Tatum, *Can We Talk About Race? And Other Conversations in an Era of School Resegregation* (Boston: Beacon Press, 2007), 58.

2. John U. Ogbu, *Black American Students in an Affluent Suburb: A Study of Academic Disengagement* (Mahwah, NJ: Lawrence Erlbaum Associates, 2003), 196–202.

3. Prudence L. Carter, "Intersecting Identities: 'Acting White,' Gender, and Academic Achievement," in *Beyond Acting White: Reframing the Debate on Black Student Achievement*, eds. Erin McNamara Horvat and Carla O'Connor (New York: Rowman & Littlefield, 2006), 131.

4. Jawanza Kunjufu, "How to Improve Academic Achievement in African American Males," *Teachers of Color*, April 2006.

5. John McWhorter, *Losing the Race: Self-Sabotage in Black America* (New York: HarperCollins, 2001), 270.

6. Maldwyn A. Jones, *The Limits of Liberty: American History 1607–1980* (New York: Oxford University Press, 1991), 255.

7. Ibid.

8. H. Richard Milner and Tyrone C. Howard, "Black Teachers, Black Students, Black Communities, and Brown: Perspectives and Insights from Experts," *Journal of Negro Education* 73, no. 3 (Summer 2004): 286.

9. Earl Ofari Hutchinson, *The Assassination of the Black Male Image* (New York: Simon & Schuster, 1996), 136.

10. James Tackach, *Brown v. Board of Education* (San Diego: Lucent Books, 1998), 45.

11. Jones, *The Limits of Liberty*, 588–589.

12. Raymond Wolters, *The Burden of Brown: Thirty Years of School Desegregation* (Knoxville: The University of Tennessee Press, 1984), 13–15, 273.

13. Chance W. Lewis, "African American Male Teachers in Public Schools: An Examination of Three Urban School Districts," *Teachers College Record* 108, no. 2 (February 2006): 227.

14. W. E. Burghardt DuBois, "Does the Negro Need Separate Schools?" *The Journal of Negro Education* 4, no. 3 (July 1935): 328, 335.

15. Ibid., 335.

16. Tatum, *Can We Talk About Race?*, 51.

17. Ibid., 29–32.

18. Susan Jacoby, *The Age of American Unreason* (New York: Pantheon Books, 2008), 237; Richard N. Ostling and Sidney Urquhart, "Is School Unfair to Girls?" *Time*, February 24, 1992.

19. Tatum, *Can We Talk About Race?*, 25–26.

20. Gary R. Howard, *We Can't Teach What We Don't Know: White Teachers, Multiracial Schools* (New York: Teachers College Press, 1999), 99.

21. Ibid.

22. Ibid., 85.

23. Ibid., 103.

24. Ibid., 107.

25. Patricia M. Cooper, "Does Race Matter? A Comparison of Effective Black and White Teachers of African American Students," in *In Search of Wholeness: African American Teachers and Their Culturally Specific Classroom Practices*, ed. Jacqueline Jordan Irvine (New York: Palgrave, 2002), 54–58.

26. Glenn E. Singleton and Curtis Linton, *Courageous Conversations About Race: A Field Guide for Achieving Equity in Schools* (Thousand Oaks, CA: Corwin Press, 2006), 38.

27. Ibid., 26.

28. Hutchinson, *Black Male*, 15, 21.

29. Ibid., 15, 21–22.

30. Ibid., 15.

31. Tatum, *Can We Talk About Race?*, 51; Singleton and Linton, *Courageous Conversations About Race*, 26–28; Ogbu, *Black American Students*, 84–85; Howard, *We Can't Teach What We Don't Know*, 85.

32. Julie Landsman, "Confronting the Racism of Low Expectations," *Educational Leadership* 62, no. 3 (November 2004): 28.

33. Ibid.

34. Cornel West, *Race Matters* (New York: Vintage Books, 2001), 5.

35. Jawanza Kunjufu, *Black Students—Middle-Class Teachers* (Chicago: African American Images, 2002), 27–30.

36. Tatum, *Can We Talk About Race?*, 51; Singleton and Linton, *Courageous Conversations About Race*, 26–28; Ogbu,

*Black American Students*, 84–85; Howard, *We Can't Teach What We Don't Know*, 85.

37. Robert Rosenthal and Lenore Jacobson, *Pygmalion in the Classroom: Teacher Expectation and Pupils' Intellectual Development* (New York: Holt, Rinehart and Winston, 1968), 176.

38. Ellis Cose, "The Black Gender Gap," *Newsweek*, March 3, 2003; Juan Williams, *Enough: The Phony Leaders, Dead-End Movements, and Culture of Failure that are Undermining Black America—and What We Can Do about It* (New York: Three Rivers Press, 2006), 94.

39. Jawanza Kunjufu, *Keeping Black Boys Out of Special Education* (Chicago: African American Images, 2005), v.

40. Ibid., 12; James C. Raines, "Improving Educational and Behavioral Performance of Students with Learning Disabilities," in *The School Services Sourcebook: A Guide for School-Based Professionals*, eds. Cynthia Franklin, Mary Beth Harris, and Paula Allen-Meares (New York: Oxford University Press, 2006), 201.

41. National Research Council, "Learning Disabilities at a Glance," National Center for Learning Disabilities, http://www.ncld.org/index.php?option=content&task=view&id=448 (accessed December 13, 2008); Kunjufu, *Keeping Black Boys Out of Special Education*, vi, 12, 16, 29.

42. Beth Harry and Mary G. Anderson, "The Disproportionate Placement of African American Males in Special Education Programs: A Critique of the Process," *The Journal of Negro Education* 63, no. 4 (Autumn 1994): 606.

43. Lori Granger and Bill Granger, *The Magic Feather: The Truth About "Special Education"* (New York: E.P. Dutton, 1986), 7.

44. Ibid., 88.

45. Kunjufu, *Keeping Black Boys Out of Special Education*, 11.

46. Sandra M. Cooley Nichols et al., "A Field at Risk: The Teacher Shortage in Special Education," *Phi Delta Kappan* 89, no. 8 (April 2008): 597–598.

47. Kunjufu, *Keeping Black Boys Out of Special Education*, 13.

48. National Education Association, *Changing the Landscape: Including Students with Disabilities in High School Graduation Rates* (Washington DC: NEA Education Policy and Practice Department, 2008), 1; National Center for Learning Disabilities, *Why Students with Learning Disabilities Need No Child Left Behind* (Washington DC: Public Policy Office, 2004), 1.

49. National Education Association, *Changing the Landscape*, 2.

50. Ibid.

## 3. The Influence of the Peer Group

1. Beverly Daniel Tatum, *Can We Talk About Race? And Other Conversations in an Era of School Resegregation* (Boston: Beacon Press, 2007), 51–52.

2. Spencer J. Salend and Laurel M. Garrick Duhaney, "Understanding and Addressing the Disproportionate Representation of Students of Color in Special Education," *Intervention in School and Clinic* 40, no. 4 (March 2005): 214.

3. Juan Williams, *Enough: The Phony Leaders, Dead-End Movements, and Culture of Failure that are Undermining Black America—and What We Can Do about It* (New York: Three

Rivers Press, 2006), 93–94; John McWhorter, *Losing the Race: Self-Sabotage in Black America* (New York: HarperCollins, 2001), 100.

4. U.S. Bureau of the Census, *Survey of Business Owners (SBO): Economy-Wide Estimate of Business Ownership by Gender, Hispanic or Latino Origin, and Race, 2002* (Washington DC: GPO, 2006); National Science Foundation, *Employed Scientists and Engineers, By Occupation, Highest Degree Level, Race/Ethnicity and Sex, 2003* (Arlington, VA: SRS, 2006); National Science Foundation, *Citizenship Status, Race/Ethnicity, and Sex of Ph.D.s, by Field of Doctorate: 1975–99 Total and 5-Year Cohorts From 1975* (Arlington, VA: SRS, 2006).

5. Joan Z. Spade and Catherine G. Valentine, *The Kaleidoscope of Gender: Prisms, Patterns, and Possibilities* (Thousand Oaks, CA: Sage Publications, Inc., 2007), 193; John U. Ogbu, *Black American Students in an Affluent Suburb: A Study of Academic Disengagement* (Mahwah, NJ: Lawrence Erlbaum Associates, 2003), 159–160.

6. Ronald B. Mincy and Hillard Pouncy, "The Marriage Mystery: Marriage, Assets, and the Expectations of African American Families," in *Black Fathers in Contemporary American Society: Strengths, Weaknesses, and Strategies for Change*, eds. Obie Clayton, Ronald B. Mincy, and David Blankenhorn (New York: Russell Sage Foundation, 2003), 51; Leon D. Caldwell and Le'Roy Reese, "The Fatherless Father: On Becoming Dad," in *Black Fathers: An Invisible Presence in America*, eds. Michael E. Connor and Joseph L. White (Mahwah, NJ: Lawrence Erlbaum Associates, 2006), 171–172; Charles Whitaker, "Do Black Males Need Special Schools?" *Ebony*, March 1991.

7. U.S. Department of Justice, *Crime in the United States: Arrests by Race, 2006* (Washington DC: GPO, 2006).

8. Child Trends Data Bank, "Percentage of Births to Unmarried Women," Child Trends, http://www.childtrendsdatabank.org/pdf/75_PDF.pdf (accessed January 19, 2009).

9. U.S. Department of Health and Human Services, *Fact Sheet: HIV/AIDS Among African Americans, 2005* (Washington DC: CDC, HIV/AIDS Reporting System, 2008); Steven Reinberg, "One in 4 Teen Girls Has a Sexually Transmitted Disease," *U.S. News & World Report*, March 11, 2008.

10. Ellis Cose, *The Envy of the World: On Being a Black Man in America* (New York: Washington Square Press, 2002), 70.

11. John U. Ogbu, "Collective Identity and the Burden of 'Acting White' in Black History, Community, and Education," *The Urban Review* 36, no. 1 (March 2004): 1–2.

12. Ibid., 19; Tatum, *Can We Talk About Race?*, 58; Ogbu, *Black American Students*, 196–202.

13. Ellis Cose, "The Black Gender Gap," *Newsweek*, March 3, 2003; Marcus A. Winters and Jay P. Greene, "Leaving Boys Behind: Public High School Graduation Rates," Manhattan Institute for Policy Research, April 2006, https://www.policyarchive.org/handle/10207/11774 (accessed January 28, 2009).

14. Joe R. Feagin and Eileen O'Brien, *White Men on Race: Power, Privilege, and the Shaping of Cultural Consciousness* (Boston: Beacon Press, 2003), 177.

15. U.S. Department of Justice, *Juvenile Arrest Rate Trends, 1980–2007* (Washington DC: OJJDP Statistical Briefing Book, 2007).

16. *Encyclopedia of Educational Psychology* (Thousand Oaks, CA: Sage Publications, Inc., 2008), s.v. "gangs."

17. *The American Heritage Dictionary*, rev. ed., s.v. "hypersexual."

18. Cornel West, *Race Matters* (New York: Vintage Books, 2001), 119.

19. U.S. Department of Health and Human Services, *2008 National STD Prevention Conference* (Washington DC: CDC, Division of STD Prevention, 2008).

20. U.S. Department of Health and Human Services, *Sexually Transmitted Diseases: STD Surveillance 2007 Tables 11A, 21A, & 33A* (Washington DC: CDC, Division of STD Prevention, 2007); Sonia Ruiz, Jennifer Kates, and Claire Oseran Pontius, *HIV/AIDS Policy Fact Sheet: African Americans and HIV/AIDS* (Washington DC: The Henry J. Kaiser Family Foundation, 2003), 1.

21. Richard Majors and Janet Mancini Billson, *Cool Pose: The Dilemmas of Black Manhood in America* (New York: Simon & Schuster, 1992), 2.

22. U.S. Department of Justice, *Prisoners in 2006* (Washington DC: BJS Publications, 2007); Gennaro F. Vito, Jeffrey R. Maahs, and Ronald M. Holmes, *Criminology: Theory, Research, and Policy*, 2nd ed. (Boston: Jones & Bartlett, 2006), 250; Chad R. Trulson, James W. Marquart, and Soraya K. Kawucha, "Gang Suppression & Institutional Control," *Corrections Today*, April 2006.

23. Michelle Fine, "Witnessing Whiteness/Gathering Intelligence," in *Off White: Readings on Power, Privilege, and Resistance*, eds. Michelle Fine et al., 2nd ed. (Florence, KY: Routledge, 2004), 252.

24. U.S. Department of Health and Human Services, *Characteristics of Incarcerated Fathers* (Washington DC: ASPE, HHS, 2008).

25. U.S. Department of Justice, *Criminal Sentencing Statistics* (Washington DC: BJS Publications, 2004); Gennaro F. Vito, Jeffrey R. Maahs, and Ronald M. Holmes, *Criminology: Theory, Research, and Policy*, 2nd ed. (Boston, MA: Jones & Bartlett, 2006), 250.

26. Stanley Tookie Williams, *Blue Rage, Black Redemption: A Memoir* (New York: Simon & Schuster, 2007), 293.

27. Absolute Astronomy, "Zoot Suit," AbsoluteAstronomy. com, http://www.absoluteastronomy.com/topics/Zoot_suit (accessed March 10, 2009); Chris Stevenson, "Why Sagging Pants are Conspicuously Still in Style," *Political Affairs Magazine*, July 25, 2008.

28. AbsoluteAstronomy, "Bell-Bottoms," AbsoluteAstronomy. com, http://www.absoluteastronomy.com/topics/Bell-bottoms (accessed March 10, 2009); Stevenson, "Sagging Pants."

29. KMOV News, "Cities Cracking Down on Saggy Pants," KMOV.com, September 17, 2007, http://www.kmov. com/justposted/stories/kmov_topstories_070917_saggypants. e1588c17. html (accessed March 21, 2009).

30. Ibid.

31. Ibid.; Lindsay M. Hayes, *Prison Suicide: An Overview and Guide to Prevention* (Darby, PA: Diane Publishing, 1995), 15–16.

32. Michael Eric Dyson, *The Michael Eric Dyson Reader* (New York: Basic Civitas Books, 2004), 416.

33. John H. McWhorter, "How Hip-Hop Holds Blacks Back," *City-Journal* 13, no. 3 (Summer 2003): 68, 75.

34. Katheryn Russell-Brown, *Underground Codes: Race, Crime, and Related Fires* (New York: New York University Press, 2004), 41.

35. McWhorter, "Hip-Hop," *City-Journal* 13, no. 3 (Summer 2003): 66.

36. Katheryn Russell-Brown, *Underground Codes: Race, Crime, and Related Fires* (New York: New York University Press, 2004), 49.

37. Stephen Prince, *A New Pot of Gold: Hollywood Under the Electronic Rainbow, 1980–1989*, vol. 10 of *History of the American Cinema* (New York: Charles Scribner's Sons, 2000), 230–231.

38. Ibid., 230.

39. The Age Company Ltd., "Scarface Refuses to Fade," Fairfax Digital, September 25, 2003, http://www.theage.com.au/articles/2003/09/24/1064083041362.html (accessed April 4, 2009).

40. MTV Networks: VH1, "Fat Joe Interview," VH1.com, September 16, 2003, http://www.vh1.com/artists/interview/1478255/09162003/fat_joe.jhtml(accessed April 4, 2009); MTV Networks: VH1, "Photo Gallery: Fat Joe," VH1.com, http://www.vh1.com/photos/gallery/?fid=611&dyn=artist&pid=3159464 (accessed April 6, 2009).

41. The Age Company Ltd., "Scarface."

42. Ibid.

43. Glenn Whipp, "The Rap on 'Scarface' Film that Wouldn't Die Now Embraced By Hip-Hop Artists as a Defining Work," *Daily News*, September 28, 2003.

44. Tiffany Danitz, "The Gangs Behind Bars," *Insight on the News*, September 28, 1998; Laura K. Egendorf, ed., *Gangs: Opposing Viewpoints* (San Diego: Greenhaven Press, 2001), 12.

45. John J. DiIulio, Jr., *Governing Prisons: A Comparative Study of Correctional Management* (New York: The Free Press, 1987), 21.

46. Florida Department of Corrections, *Major Prison Gangs: Gang and Security Threat Group Awareness* (Tallahassee: Bureau of Research and Data Analysis, 1992).

47. Rufus Schatzberg and Robert J. Kelly, *African American Organized Crime: A Social History* (Piscataway, NJ: Rutgers University Press, 1997), 195.

48. John J. Conrad et al., *Juvenile Justice: A Guide to Theory, Policy, and Practice*, 6th ed. (Thousand Oaks, CA: Sage Publications, Inc., 2007), 290–291.

49. Derrick Watkins and Richard Ashby, *Gang Investigations: A Street Cop's Guide* (Boston, MA: Jones & Bartlett, 2006), 24.

50. U.S. Department of Justice, *National Youth Gang Survey Analysis: Demographics, 2001–2004* (Washington DC: Office of Juvenile Justice and Delinquency Prevention, 2007).

51. Ibid.

52. *The American Heritage Book of English Usage* (Boston: Houghton Mifflin, 1996), s.v. "Negro."

53. Hosea Easton, *A Treatise on the Intellectual Character and Civil and Political Condition of the Colored People of the United States: and the Prejudice Exercised Toward Them* (Boston: Isaac Knapp Publishing, 1837), 40.

54. *Random House Historical Dictionary of American Slang* (New York: Random House, 1997), s.v. "nigger"; *Cassell's Dictionary of Slang* (New York: Sterling, 2005), s.v. "nigger."

55. Margaret M. Russell, "Beyond 'Sellouts' and 'Race Cards': Black Attorneys and the Straitjacket of Legal Practice," *Michigan Law Review* 95 (February 1997): 765.

56. Jabari Asim, *The N Word: Who Can Say It, Who Shouldn't, and Why* (New York: Houghton Mifflin, 2007), 10.

57. Ibid.

58. Randall Kennedy, *Nigger: The Strange Career of a Troublesome Word* (New York: Vintage Books, 2003), 5–7.

59. *Random House Historical Dictionary of American Slang* (New York: Random House, 1997), s.v.v. "nigger baby," "nigger bean," "niggerish," "nigger-knocker," "nigger news," "nigger out," "nigger-shooter."

60. *Towne v. Eisner*, 245 U.S. 418 (1918).

61. Metroleap Media Inc., Searchable Lyrics Database, http://www.metrolyrics.com/ (accessed April 30, 2009).

62. Ibid.

63. Ibid.

64. Ibid.

65. Ibid.

66. Ibid.

67. RealTalkNY, "Top 10 Selling Rap Albums in 2008," http://realtalkny.uproxx.com/2009/01/topic/new/top-10-selling-rap-albums-in-2008/ (accessed April 30, 2009).

68. Kennedy, *Nigger*, 138.

69. Ed Morales, *The Latin Beat: The Rhythms and Roots of Latin Music from Bossa Nova to Salsa and Beyond* (New York: Da Capo Press, 2003), 163.

70. Kennedy, *Nigger*, 40–41.

71. McWhorter, *Losing the Race*, vii.

72. Williams, *Enough*, 220.

73. Roger Bruns, *Jesse Jackson: A Biography* (Westport, CT: Greenwood Publishing Group, 2005), 5–8.

## 4. The Influence of the Mass Media

1. Jon M. Shepard and Robert W. Greene, *Sociology and You* (Columbus, OH: Glencoe/McGraw-Hill, 2003), 124.

2. *A Modern Dictionary of Sociology* (New York: Thomas Y. Crowell Company, 1969), s.v. "mass media."

3. Frederick Elkin and Gerald Handel, *The Child and Society: The Process of Socialization*, 3rd ed. (New York: Random House, 1978), 161.

4. Earl Ofari Hutchinson, *The Assassination of the Black Male Image* (New York: Simon & Schuster, 1996), 163.

5. Ibid., 22–23.

6. James O. Horton and Lois E. Horton, *Slavery and the Making of America* (New York: Oxford University Press, 2005), 7.

7. Winthrop D. Jordan, *The White Man's Burden: Historical Origins of Racism in the United States* (New York: Oxford University Press, 1974), 3–6.

8. Ibid., 4–6.

9. Ibid., 10–18.

10. George N. Gordon, *The Communications Revolution: A History of Mass Media in the United States* (New York: Hastings House, 1977), 18; Richard D. Brown, *Knowledge is Power: The Diffusion of Information in Early America, 1700–1865* (New York: Oxford University Press, 1989), 12.

11. Jordon, *The White Man's Burden*, 52–54.

12. Mason I. Lowance, Jr., ed., *A House Divided: The Antebellum Slavery Debates in America, 1776–1865* (Princeton, NJ: Princeton University Press, 2003), 10.

13. Ibid., 11, 14–15.

14. Edward L. Bond, ed., *Spreading the Gospel in Colonial Virginia: Sermons and Devotional Writings* (Lanham, MD: Lexington Books, 2004), 441.

15. Patricia Bradley, *Slavery, Propaganda, and the American Revolution* (Jackson, MS: University Press of Mississippi, 1998), 1.

16. Maldwyn A. Jones, *The Limits of Liberty: American History 1607–1980* (New York: Oxford University Press, 1991), 20; Gordon, *The Communications Revolution*, 15.

17. Horton and Horton, *Slavery and the Making of America*, 41; Gordon, *The Communications Revolution*, 15.

18. Jones, *The Limits of Liberty*, 61; Horton and Horton, *Slavery and the Making of America*, 49–51.

19. Richard D. Brown, *Knowledge is Power: The Diffusion of Information in Early America, 1700–1865* (New York: Oxford University Press, 1989), 12; Gordon, *The Communications Revolution*, 15, 18.

20. Bradley, *Slavery, Propaganda*, 8, 10, 26.

21. Ibid., 8.

22. Gordon, *The Communications Revolution*, 21.

23. Bradley, *Slavery, Propaganda*, 12–13, 26–27, 40–42.

24. Jordon, *The White Man's Burden*, 125–126.

25. Horton and Horton, *Slavery and the Making of America*, 64–66.

26. Jordon, *The White Man's Burden*, 125–126.

27. Ibid., 125; Jones, *The Limits of Liberty*, 76; Horton and Horton, *Slavery and the Making of America*, 67.

28. Willard W. Cochrane, *The Development of American Agriculture: A Historical Analysis*, 2nd ed. (Minneapolis, MN: University of Minnesota Press, 1993), 70; John B. Boles, *Black*

*Southerners, 1619–1869* (Lexington, KY: University Press of Kentucky, 1983), 75; Horton and Horton, *Slavery and the Making of America*, 71, 83; Jordon, *The White Man's Burden*, 127.

29. Larry E. Tise, *Proslavery: A History of the Defense of Slavery in America, 1701–1840* (Athens, GA: University of Georgia Press, 1987), 126–128.

30. Dickson D. Bruce, Jr., *The Origins of African American Literature, 1680–1865* (Charlottesville, VA: University of Virginia Press, 2001), 113; Jeffrey Robert Young, ed., *Proslavery and Sectional Thought in the Early South, 1740–1829: An Anthology* (Columbia, SC: University of South Carolina Press, 2006), 173–174.

31. Young, *Proslavery and Sectional Thought*, 198–200.

32. John Patrick Daly, *When Slavery Was Called Freedom: Evangelicalism, Proslavery, and the Causes of the Civil War* (Lexington, KY: University Press of Kentucky, 2004), 36; Fergus M. Bordewich, *Bound for Canaan: The Underground Railroad and the War for the Soul of America* (New York: HarperCollins, 2005), 105–107.

33. Lowance, Jr., *A House Divided*, 62–63, 67.

34. Jay R. Mandle, "Black Economic Entrapment after Emancipation in the United States," in *The Meaning of Freedom: Economics, Politics, and Culture after Slavery*, eds. Frank McGlynn and Seymour Drescher (Pittsburgh, PA: University of Pittsburgh Press, 1992), 72.

35. Eric Foner, *Reconstruction: America's Unfinished Revolution, 1863–1877* (New York: Harper & Row, 1988), 425; Ronda Racha Penrice, *African American History for Dummies* (Hoboken, NJ: Wiley, 2007), 108.

36. Jones, *The Limits of Liberty*, 258–259; Penrice, *African American History*, 116–118.

37. Clint C. Wilson II, Felix Gutierrez, and Lena M. Chao, *Racism, Sexism, and the Media: The Rise of Class Communication in Multicultural America*, 3rd ed. (Thousand Oaks, CA: Sage Publications, Inc., 2003), 73.

38. Ibid.

39. *The Encyclopedia of New York City* (New Haven, CT: Yale University Press, 1995), s.v. "minstrelsy."

40. Jones, *The Limits of Liberty*, 268–269.

41. *History of the Mass Media in the United States: An Encyclopedia* (Chicago: Fitzroy Dearborn, 1998), s.v. "mass media and race"; Hutchinson, *The Assassination of the Black Male Image*, 22.

42. *History of the Mass Media in the United States*, s.v. "mass media and race."

43. Wilson II, Gutierrez, and Chao, *Racism, Sexism, and the Media*, 73–74.

44. Jones, *The Limits of Liberty*, 317–318; *The Columbia Encyclopedia*, 3rd ed. (New York: Columbia University Press, 1963), s.v. "Industrial Revolution"; Edwin Emery, *The Press and America: An Interpretative History of the Mass Media*, 3rd ed. (Englewood, NJ: Prentice-Hall, Inc., 1972), 381–382.

45. *Encyclopedia of African-American Culture and History* (New York: Simon & Schuster Macmillan, 1996), s.v. "economics."

46. Ibid.; R. Douglas Hurt, ed., *African American Life in the Rural South, 1900–1950* (Columbia, MO: University of Missouri Press, 2003), 1.

47. Leonard Broom and Norval D. Glenn, *Transformation of the Negro American* (New York: Harper & Row Publishers, 1965), 83; Jones, *The Limits of Liberty*, 268–269.

48. Penrice, *African American History*, 124.

49. Frank J. McVeigh and Loreen Wolfer, *Brief History of Social Problems: A Critical Thinking Approach* (Lanham, MD: Rowman & Littlefield, 2004), 134.

50. William P. Pickett, *The Negro Problem: Abraham Lincoln's Solution* (New York: The Knickerbocker Press, 1909), 456–457.

51. Charles A. Ellwood, "Reviews," *The American Journal of Sociology* 11, no. 4 (January 1906): 570–571.

52. Robert W. Shufeldt, *The Negro: A Menace to American Civilization* (Boston: The Gorham Press, 1907), 124–125.

53. Hutchinson, *The Assassination of the Black Male Image*, 28.

54. Ibid., 24, 28; Clint C. Wilson II and Felix Gutierrez, *Race, Multiculturalism, and the Media: From Mass to Class Communications*, 2nd ed. (Thousand Oaks, CA: Sage Publications,Inc., 1995), 114–117.

55. *History of the Mass Media in the United States*, s.v. "Birth of a Nation, The"; Wilson II, Gutierrez, and Chao, *Racism, Sexism, and the Media*, 76.

56. Corin Willis, "Meaning and Value in the Jazz Singer (Alan Crosland, 1927)," in *Style and Meaning: Studies in the Detailed Analysis of Film*, eds. John Gibbs and Douglas Pye (Manchester, UK: Manchester University Press, 2005), 127–130; Wilson II, Gutierrez, and Chao, *Racism, Sexism, and the Media*, 74–75.

57. Wilson II, Gutierrez, and Chao, *Racism, Sexism, and the Media*, 80–82.

58. Ibid., 78.

59. Ibid., 119; Hutchinson, *The Assassination of the Black Male Image*, 72; Marilyn Kern-Foxworth, *Aunt Jemima, Uncle Ben, and Rastus: Blacks in Advertising, Yesterday, Today, and Tomorrow* (Westport, CT: Greenwood Press, 1994), 38–41.

60. Jones, *The Limits of Liberty*, 554; Paul R. Spickard, *Mixed Blood: Intermarriage and Ethnic Identity in Twentieth-Century America* (Madison, WI: University of Wisconsin Press, 1991), 286–287; Wilson II, Gutierrez, and Chao, *Racism, Sexism, and the Media*, 119.

61. Jones, *The Limits of Liberty*, 581.

62. *Loving v. Virginia*, 388 U.S. 1 (1967).

63. Gerald David Jaynes and Robin M. Williams, Jr., eds., *A Common Destiny: Blacks and American Society* (Washington DC: National Academy Press, 1989), 120.

64. NAA Business Analysis & Research Department, "Daily Newspaper Readership Trend—Total Adults (1964–1997)," Newspaper Association of America, http://www.naa.org/ TrendsandNumbers/Readership.aspx (accessed August 28, 2009); Photius Coutsoukis and Information Technology Associates, "Daily and Sunday Newspapers – Number and Circulation," Allcountries.org, http://www.allcountries.org/uscensus/932_ daily_and_sunday_newspapers_number_and.html (accessed August 28, 2009).

65. *History of the Mass Media in the United States*, s.v. "magazines of the twentieth century."

66. Edwin Emery, *The Press and America: An Interpretative History of the Mass Media*, 3rd ed. (Englewood, NJ: Prentice-Hall, 1972), 599–600; *Encyclopedia Americana* (Danbury, CT: Grolier Incorporated, 1999), s.v. "radio."

67. *The New Encyclopaedia Britannica*, 15th ed. (Chicago: Encyclopaedia Britannica, Inc., 2005), s.v. "motion picture."

68. D. Garth Taylor, Paul B. Sheatsley, and Andrew M. Greeley, "Attitudes Toward Racial Integration," *Scientific American* 238, no. 6 (June 1978): 42–44.

69. Jaynes and Williams, Jr., eds., *A Common Destiny*, 120.

70. Ibid., 155.

71. Ibid., 121, 124, 155.

72. Robert W. Fairlie and Alexandra M. Resch, "Is There 'White Flight' Into Private Schools? Evidence from the National Educational Longitudinal Survey," *The Review of Economics and Statistics* 84, no. 1 (February 2002): 32.

73. Jesse Algeron Rhines, *Black Film/White Money* (New Brunswick, NJ: Rutgers University Press, 2000), 43–45.

74. Ibid., 44–45.

75. Ibid., 51.

76. U.S. Bureau of the Census, *Poverty Status of People by Family Relationship, Race, and Hispanic Origin: 1959 to 2006* (Washington DC: HHES Division, 2009).

77. Paul A. Jargowsky, *Poverty and Place: Ghettos, Barrios, and the American City* (New York: Russell Sage Foundation, 1997), 38–39; Faye Z. Belgrave and Kevin W. Allison, *African American Psychology: From Africa to America* (Thousand Oaks, CA: Sage Publications, Inc., 2006), 112.

78. Martin Gilens, *Why Americans Hate Welfare: Race, Media, and the Politics of Antipoverty Policy* (Chicago: University of Chicago Press, 1999), 114–115, 121.

79. Ibid., 128.

80. Clarence Page, *Showing My Color: Impolite Essays on Race and Identity* (New York: Harper Collins Publishers, 1996), 242;

Dan T. Carter, *From George Wallace to Newt Gingrich: Race in the Conservative Counterrevolution 1963–1994* (Baton Rouge, LA: Louisiana State University Press, 1996), 14.

81. Jones, *The Limits of Liberty*, 557–558, 651.

82. Kenneth O'Reilly, *Nixon's Piano: Presidents and Racial Politics from Washington to Clinton* (New York: Simon & Schuster, 1995), 281, 360–361.

83. Ibid., 381–382.

84. Ibid., 420.

85. Ibid., 244.

86. Travis L. Dixon, "Network News and Racial Beliefs: Exploring the Connection between National Television News Exposure and Stereotypical Perceptions of African Americans," *Journal of Communication* 58, no. 2 (July 2008): 331–332.

87. Ibid., 332; Mary Beth Oliver et al., "The Face of Crime: Viewers' Memory of Race-Related Facial Features of Individuals Pictured in the News," *Journal of Communication* 54, no. 1 (March 2004): 99.

88. Wilson II and Gutierrez, *Race, Multiculturalism, and the Media*, 53–54.

## Conclusion: Why Our Black Boys Choose Enslavement

1. U.S. Department of Justice, *Juvenile Arrest Rate Trends, 1980–2007* (Washington DC: OJJDP Statistical Briefing Book, 2007).

2. U.S. Department of Justice, *Lifetime Likelihood of Going to State or Federal Prison, 2001* (Washington DC: BJS Publications, 2008).

3. U.S. Department of Justice, *Black Victims of Violent Crime, 2005* (Washington DC: BJS Publications, 2007).

4. Ronald E. Hall and Jesenia M. Pizarro, "Unemployment as Conduit of Black Self-Hate: Pathogenic Rates of Black Male Homicide via Legacy of the Antebellum," *Journal of Black Studies* 38, no. 5 (May 2008).

5. Ibid.

6. Alvin F. Poussaint, "Building a Strong Self-Image in the Black Child," *Ebony*, August 1974; Jocelyn Emama Maxime, "The Therapeutic Importance of Racial Identity in Working with Black Children Who Hate," in *How and Why Children Hate: A Study of Conscious and Unconscious Sources*, ed. Ved Varma (London, UK: Jessica Kingsley Publishers, 1993), 99.

7. Jon M. Shepard and Robert W. Greene, *Sociology and You* (Columbus, OH: Glencoe/McGraw-Hill, 2003), 30–31, 116–117; Charles Horton Cooley, *Human Nature and the Social Order* (New York: Charles Scribner's Sons, 1902); George Herbert Mead, *Mind, Self and Society: From the Standpoint of a Social Behaviorist* (Chicago: University of Chicago Press, 1934).

8. *Encyclopedia of Human Behavior* (San Diego: Academic Press, 1994), s.v. "self-esteem."

9. Larry E. Davis, "Perspectives: A Gender Gap in Black and White," *Pittsburgh Post-Gazette*, July 29, 2003.

10. Claude M. Steele, "Thin Ice: Stereotype Threat and Black College Students," *Atlantic Monthly*, August 1999.

11. Beverly Daniel Tatum, *Can We Talk About Race? And Other Conversations in an Era of School Resegregation* (Boston: Beacon Press, 2007), 60.

12. Diana Kendall, *Sociology in Our Times: The Essentials*, 7th ed. (Belmont, CA: Wadsworth Cengage Learning, 2007), 90–91;

Shepard and Greene, *Sociology*, 118–119; George Herbert Mead, *Mind, Self and Society: From the Standpoint of a Social Behaviorist* (Chicago: University of Chicago Press, 1934).

13. Kathleen D. Vohs and Roy F. Baumeister, "Understanding Self-Regulation: An Introduction," in *Handbook of Self-Regulation: Research, Theory, and Applications*, eds. Roy F. Baumeister and Kathleen D. Vohs (New York: The Guilford Press, 2004), 1–2.

14. Joan E. LeFebvre, *Parenting the Preschooler: Self-Regulation* (Eagle River, WI: University of Wisconsin, Extension, 2003).

15. Susan Golombok, *Parenting: What Really Counts?* (Florence, KY: Routledge, 2000), 5; George R. Taylor, *Practical Application of Social Learning Theories in Educating Young African-American Males* (Lanham, MD: University Press of America, 2003), 38–39; Josef A. Passley, Joan P. Gerring, and Arlene C. Gerson, "The Relationship between Paternal Involvement and Child Outcomes in Male African American Youth," Forum on Public Policy, 2006, http://www.forumonpublicpolicy.com/archive07/passley.pdf (accessed November 13, 2009).

16. Don Martin et al., "Increasing Prosocial Behavior and Academic Achievement among Adolescent African American Males," *Adolescence* 42, no. 168 (Winter 2007): 689–690.

17. U.S. Department of Justice, *Crime in the United States: Arrests by Race, 2006* (Washington DC: GPO, 2006).

18. Child Trends Data Bank, "Percentage of Births to Unmarried Women," Child Trends, http://www.childtrendsdatabank.org/pdf/75_PDF.pdf (accessed January 19, 2009); U.S. Department of Health and Human Services, *Fact Sheet: HIV/AIDS Among African Americans, 2005* (Washington DC: CDC, HIV/AIDS Reporting System, 2008); Steven Reinberg, "One in 4 Teen Girls

Has a Sexually Transmitted Disease," *U.S. News & World Report*, March 11, 2008.

19. Michael S. Kimmel, "Masculinity as Homophobia: Fear, Shame, and Silence in the Construction of Gender Identity," in *Gender Relations in Global Perspective: Essential Readings*, ed. Nancy Cook (Toronto, ON: Canadian Scholars' Press), 73.

20. Ibid.

21. *American Masculinities: A Historical Encyclopedia* (Thousand Oaks, CA: Sage Publications, Inc., 2003), s.v. "African-American manhood."

22. Mark Roth, "Sociologist Suggests Ways to Get Fathers More Involved with Kids," *Pittsburgh Post-Gazette*, April 6, 2006.

23. Byron Hurt, "Redefining Black Manhood," in *The Black Male Handbook: A Blueprint for Life*, ed. Kevin Powell (New York: Atria Books, 2008), 53–54.

24. Jawanza Kunjufu, *Countering the Conspiracy to Destroy Black Boys* (Chicago: African American Images, 1985), 27.

25. Ibid.

26. Jeffrey M. Jones, "Majority of Americans Say Racism Against Blacks Widespread," *USA Today*/Gallup Poll, August 4, 2008, http://www.gallup.com/poll/109258/majority-americans-say-racism-against-blacks-widespread.aspx (accessed November 16, 2009).

27. CNN Staff, "Poll: Most Americans See Lingering Racism—In Others," Cable News Network, December 12, 2006, http://www.cnn.com/2006/US/12/12/racism.poll/index.html (accessed August 4, 2008).

28. U.S. Department of Justice, *Correctional Populations in the United States, 1993* (Washington DC: BJS Publications, 1995).

29. *Encyclopedia of Psychology*, s.v.v. "self-esteem," "self-regulation."

30. *The Blackwell Encyclopedia of Social Psychology* (Malden, MA: Blackwell Publishing, 1996), s.v. "self-esteem."

# Index

DuBois, W. E. B., 55, 56, 121, 130, 153
Dukakis, Michael, 117
Dyson, Michael Eric, 123, 141, 160

# E

Easton, Hosea, 89, 162
Edgar, Kimmett, 18, 144
education. *See also* academic achievement; academic expectations; school systems; special education; teachers
  all-black, all-male schools, 36
  blacks hungry for, 51–52, 53
  blacks shifting away from, 55
  as feminine thing, 36, 40, 49, 50, 53, 55, 71, 123
  of the mother, 30
  as white thing, 40, 49, 50, 51, 71
*Education for All Handicapped Children Act* (Public Law 94-142), 66, 69
Egypt, 4
Eighth Amendment, 15
Elders, Jocelyn, 44
EME (Mexican Mafia), 85, 86
Eminem (white rapper), 92
*Encyclopedia of Educational Psychology*, 77, 158
*Encyclopedia of Human Behavior*, 124
*The Encyclopedia of New York City*, 105, 167
*Encyclopedia of Psychology*, 125, 138, 175

*Encyclopedia of Sociology*, 33
*Enough* (Williams), 44, 151, 155, 156, 163
enslavement
  as choice, ix, 4, 24, 121, 137, 138
  compared to incarceration, 21–22
  rationale for, 3, 13
  as synonymous with black, 98
entertainers. *See also* blackface acts; *specific names*, as role models for black males, 35, 39–40, 82
entertainment
  associated with black masculinity, 123
  as blind obsession, 126
  minstrelsy, 105
environmentally induced pathologies, 23–24
*The Envy of the World* (Cose), 74, 158
"Everything" (Young Jeezy), 91
ex-cons, influence of, 80, 82, 130, 131
expectancy advantage, 64
extreme machismo, 24, 46

# F

failure
  academically, 57, 63, 75
  as choice, ix, 138
  cycle of, 73
  feelings of, 46
  as outcome for following peer group, 94

self-regulation, 32–33, 128, 129
separate but equal doctrine, 43, 53, 106
Sewall, Samuel, 89
sexual stereotypes
    of black males, 77. *See also* hypersexuality
    of blacks, 60, 78
    of whites, 135
sexuality, impact on black male attitudes toward education, 50
*Showing My Color* (Page), 116, 170
Shufeldt, Robert W., 107, 108, 168
Simmons, Ruth, 44
Simpson, O. J., 89
Simsburg dungeon, 20
Singleton, Glenn E., 60, 154
Sister Soulijah (rap star), 117
sitcoms, 135
skin color, 121
slave, etymology of word, 10–11
slave trade
    African, 9, 10, 12, 89, 97
    international illegal, 10
slavery
    authentic slave system, 8, 14
    in Babylon, Mesopotamia, 6–7
    characteristics of, 11–12, 13, 14, 15, 18
    chattel slavery, 3, 6, 8, 9, 103
    defense of using Biblical principles, 103
    defined, 13
    historical comparison of, 8

irrational attachment to, 3–4
    and mass media, 98, 99, 100, 101, 102, 103, 108
    plebian, 3, 8
    of the twenty-first century, 8, 9
slaves, as property, 6, 8
Slavs, 10
slow learners, as label for black males, 36
Smith, William B., 107, 108
Snoop Dog (gangsta rapper), 84
social communication skills, 32, 47
social control, 12, 13, 16, 18
social fathers, 37, 38–39
sociocultural agent, television network news as, 118
socioemotional maintenance, 31, 127
Soledad State Prison, 86
*South-Carolina Gazette*, 100
Southern blacks, 41–42, 43, 104
Southern states
    and 1968 election, 117
    employment of blacks in, 107
    and Jim Crow laws, 106
    and sense of self-righteousness, 103
    undermining of national legislation by, 41
    violence in, 104
Southern whites, during post-Reconstruction period, 61
special education
    black males as poster boys for, 124
    black males in, 69

www.ingramcontent.com/pod-product-compliance
Lightning Source LLC
Chambersburg PA
CBHW030319290526
45785CB00001B/426